Plato Redivivus
by Henry Neville

Address:
HardPress
8345 NW 66TH ST #2561
MIAMI FL 33166-2626
USA
Email: info@hardpress.net

PLATO REDIVIVVS
OR A DIALOGVE CONCERNING GOVERNMENT

Wherein, by obfervations drawn from other Kingdoms and States, both ancient and modern, an endeavour is ufed to difcover the prefent politic diftemper of our own; with the caufes and remedies.

BY HENRY NEVILLE

NON EGO SVM VATES SED PRISCI CONSCIVS AEVI
PLVRIBVS EXEMPLIS HAEC TIBI MYSTA CANQ
RES NOLVNT MALE ADMINISTRARI

The fourth edition.
London, printed for A. Millar,
MDCCLXIII

SOME ACCOVNT OF H. NEVILLE

Henry Neville, fecond fon of Sir Henry Neville, of Billingbeare in Berks, knight, was educated at Oxford.

In the beginning of the civil war, he travelled into Italy and other countries, whereby he advanced himfelf much as to the knowledge of modern languages and men; and returning in 1645 or thereabout, became Recruiter in the Long Parlament for Abingdon in Berkfhire, at which time he was very intimate with Harry Marten, Thomas Chaloner, Thomas Scot, James Harrington, and other zealous Commonwealths men.

In Nov. 1651, he was elected one of the Council of State, being then a favorite of Oliver; but when he faw that Perfon gaped after the government by a fingle Perfon, he left him, was out of his favor, and acted little during his government.

In 1658 he was elected burgefs for Reading, to ferve in Richard's Parlament, and

when

when that Perſon was depoſed and the Long Parlament ſhortly after reſtored, he was again elected one of the Council of State.

———— He was a great Rota-man, was one of the chief perſons of James Harrington's club of commonwealths men, to inſtil their principles into others, he being eſteemed to be a man of good parts, and a well-bred gentleman. At the appearance of "The "Commonwealth of Oceana," which for the practicableneſs, equality, and compleatneſs of it, is the moſt perfect form of ſuch a government that ever was delineated by any antient or modern pen, it was greedily bought up, and coming into the hands of Thomas Hobbes of Malmeſbury, he would often ſay, that Harry Neville had a finger in that pye, and thoſe that knew them both were of the ſame opinion. By that book, and both their ſmart diſcourſes and inculcations daily in Coffee houſes, they obtained many proſelytes. In 1659, in the beginning of Michaelmaſs term, they had every night a meeting at the then Turk's head, in New Palace Yard, Weſtminſter, called Miles's

Miles's Coffee houſe, to which place their Diſciples and Virtuoſi would commonly repair ; and their diſcourſes about government and ordering of a Commonwealth, were the moſt ingenious and ſmart that ever were heard, the arguments in the Parlament Houſe being but flat to thoſe. They had a balloting box, and balloted how things ſhould be carried by way of Tentamens, which not being uſed or known in England before, on that account, the room every evening was very full. Beſide the author and Harry Neville, who were the prime men of this Club, were Cyriac Skinner, a merchant's Son of London, an ingenious Young Gentleman, a ſcholar to John Milton, which Skinner ſometimes held the Chair, Major John Wildman, Charles Wolſeley of Staffordſhire, Roger Coke, William Poultney, afterward a knight, who ſometimes held the Chair, John Hoſkyns, John Aubrey, Maximilian Pettie of Tetſworth in Oxfordſhire, a very able man in theſe matters and who had more than once turned the Council board

of

of O. Cromwell, Michael Mallet, Philip Carteret of the Isle of Guernsey, Francis Cradock, a merchant, Henry Ford, Major Venner, Thomas Marriett of Warwickshire, Henry Croone, Physician, Edward Bagshaw of Christ Church and Robert Wood of Lincoln College, Oxford, James Arderne, then or soon after a Divine, with many others; beside auditors and antagonists of note. Dr. William Pettie was a Rota-man. The Doctrine was very taking, and the more, as there was no probability of the king's return. The greatest of the Parlament men hated this design of rotation and balloting, as being against their power. Eight or ten were for it, of which number Harry Neville was one, who proposed it to the House, and made it out to the Members thereof, that except they embraced that way of Government they would be ruined. The Model of it was, that the third part of the Senate or House should rote out by ballot every year, so that every third year the Senate would be wholly altered. No magistrate

trate was to continue above three Years, and all to be chosen by ballot, than which nothing could be invented more fair and impartial, as was then thought, though opposed by many for several reasons. This Club of Commonwealths men lasted till about feb. 21, 1659; at which time the secluded Members being restored by Monke, all their models vanished.

At the Restoration, he absconded; but being seized, was, among others, imprisoned, though soon after set at Liberty.

He published,

The Parlament of Ladies: Or divers remarkable Passages of Ladies in Spring Garden, in Parlament assembled. Printed 1647, in two sheets in quarto. Soon after was published, " The Ladies, a second " time, assembled in Parlament. A conti- " nuation of the Parlament of Ladies," etc. Printed 1647, in two sheets in quarto, written, as was thought, by the same hand.

Shuffling, cutting, and dealing, in a Game at Piquet, being acted from the year 1653 to 1658, by Oliver, Protector, and

and others. etc. Printed 1659, in one
sheet, in quarto.

The Isle of Pines : Or a late discovery of
a fourth Island near Terra australis incog-
nita. By Hen. Cornelius Van Sloetten. etc.
Printed, London, 1668, in four sheets and
a half in quarto. This, when first published, was looked upon as a meer piece of
Drollery.

Plato Redivivus : Or a Dialogue concerning Government, wherein, by Obser-
vations drawn from other Kingdoms and
States, both ancient and modern, an endeavour is used to discover the present politic
distemper of our own ; with the Causes and
Remedies. Printed, London, 1681, in
small octavo. This Book, which was first
published in the month of october 1680,
against the resitting of Parlament, was
very much bought up by the members
thereof and admired. It came out soon
after, in the same year 1681, " with ad-
" ditions." ——— Plato Redivivus and the
Oceana are both founded on one and
the same political maxim, that of Empire's
always following the Ballance of Property.
But

But there is this considerable difference in those works, viz. that the Oceana is only an imaginary scheme for a Commonwealth; whereas Plato Redivivus contains in it, the method of rendering a Monarchy, and particularly the monarchy of Great Britan, both happy at home and powerful abroad: the means for which are proposed distinctly and fully in the concluding Dialogue of that work. The Characters of the Persons engaged in those Dialogues are real. The Stranger, was a Nobleman of Venice, who had gone through several offices in that State; the English Gentleman is Harry Neville himself; and the Physician his great friend the celebrated Doctor Lower.

He likewise translated Machiavell's works, which were printed at London, in English, 1674 and 1680, in folio; wrote the preface to them; and first published and translated a Letter of Machiavell's, the much aspersed Nicolo Machiavelli, to Zanobio Buondelmonti, in vindication of himself and of his writings, brought by him from Italy, in 1645, on his return from his Travels.

He

He hath alfo written divers copies of verfes, which are printed in feveral books ; and was efteemed a good Poet : but as for that Pamphlet called his " Poetic Offering," to which came out " The anfwer of Ed- " ward Colman's Ghoft," printed, in one fheet, in folio, at London, in december, 1678, it is not his, but fathered on him.

This accomplifhed, faithful, magnanimous Englifhman, Henry Neville, died fept. 20, 1694, and was buried at Warfield, in Berk-fhire. Reader, fhouldft thou pafs that way, ftrew Oak Leaves on his Tomb !

THE
PUBLISHER
TO THE
READER.

Courteous READER,

*A*LL *the account I can give thee of this piece, is; that about the middle of October last it was sent to me: accompanied with a letter without a name, and written in a hand altogether unknown to me; tho' different from the character of the dialogue itself, and the argument. The letter was very short; and contained only, that the writer having the fortune to meet with this discourse, (of which he denied to be the author,) he thought it very fit to be sent to me; to the end, if I thought it could*

be of any advantage to me and no prejudice, I might publish it if I pleased and
make my best of it.   When I had open'd
it, and perceived that it treated of government, and of the present times ;   I
(supposing it to be something of the nature of those scurrilous libels, which the
press spawns every day) was extreamly
displeased with my servant, for receiving
in my absence and in these dangerous days,
such a packet ; without taking any account or notice of the messenger who
brought it : till he, to appease me, as-
sured me, that the bearer did look like a
gentleman, and had a very unsuitable
garb to a trapan, and that he did believe he had seen him often at my shop,
and that I knew him well. When I had
begun to read it, and found no harm ; I
was resolved to peruse it in the company
of a gentleman, a worthy friend of mine:
who, to his exact skill and learning in
the laws of his country, hath added a
very profound knowledge in all other li-
terature ; and particularly the excellence
of Platonick philosophy. When we had
jointly

jointly gone through it, he was clearly of opinion; that altho' some might be angry with certain passages in it, yet the discourse reflecting upon no particular person, was very uncapable of bringing me into any danger for publishing it; either from the state, or from any private man. When I had secured myself against damnum emergens; *we went about the consideration of the other part of the distinction of the schools, which is* lucrum cessans: *and I made some objections against the probability of vending this dialogue to profit; which, in things of my trade, is always my design, as it ought to be. My first fear in that behalf was; that this author would disgust the reader, in being too confident and positive in matters of so high a speculation. My friend replied; that the assurance he shewed was void of all sawciness, and expressed with great modesty: and that he verily believed, that he meant very faithfully and sincerely towards the interest of England. My next doubt was; that a considerable part of this*

treatise

treatife being a repetition of a great many principles and pofitions out of Oceana, the author would be difcredited for borrowing from another and the fale of the book hindred. To that my friend made anfwer ; that before ever Oceana came out, there were very many treatifes and pamphlets which alledged the political principle, that empire was founded in property, and difcourfed rationally upon it : Amongft the reft, one entituled A letter from an Officer in Ireland, to his highnefs the Lord Protector (which he then fhewed me) printed in 1653, as I remember ; which was more than three years before Oceana was written ; and yet, faid he, no man will aver that the learned gentleman who writ that book had ftolen from that pamphlet : For whofoever fets himfelf to ftudy politicks, muft do it by reading hiftory, and obferving in it the feveral turns and revolutions of government ; and then the caufe of fuch change will be fo vifible and obvious, that we need not impute theft to any man that finds it out : it

being

being as lawful and as easy for any person,
as well as for the author of Oceana, or
that pamphlet, to read Thucydides, Poly-
bius, Livy or Plutarch ; and if he do
so with attentiveness, he shall be sure to
find the same things there that they have
found. And if this were not lawful,
when that any one person has written in
any science, no man must write after him ;
for in polity, the orders of Government ;
in Architecture, the several orders of
Pillars, Arches, Architraves, Cornishes,
&c ; in Physick, the Causes, Prognosticks
and Crisis of Diseases, are so exactly
the same in all writers ; that we may
as well accuse all subsequent authors to
have been but plagiaries of the antecedent.
Besides this the learned gentleman added :
that Oceana was written (it being
thought lawful so to do in those times)
to evince out of these principles, that
England was not capable of any other
Government than a Democracy ; and this
author out of the same maxims or apho-
risms of politicks, endeavours to prove,
that they may be applied naturally and
fitly

fitly to the redreſſing and ſupporting one of the beſt Monarchies in the World, which is that of England.   I had but one doubt more, and that was an objection againſt the title; which I reſolved, at the firſt, not to mention; becauſe I could ſalve it by altering the title page :   But ſince I had opportunity, I acquainted the gentleman with it; and it was, that certainly no man would ever buy a book that had in the front of it ſo inſolent and preſumptuous a motto, as Plato Redivivus; *for that he muſt needs be thought not only vain in the higheſt degree, but void of ſenſe and judgment too, who compares himſelf with* Plato; *the greateſt Philoſopher, the greateſt Politician (I had almoſt ſaid the greateſt Divine too) that ever lived. My Counſellor told me, that he had as great a reſentment of any injury done to* Plato *as I, as any man could have : but that he was hard to believe, that this man intended to compare himſelf to* Plato, *either in natural parts or learning; but only to ſhew that he did imitate his*

way

way of writing, as to the manner of it,
(though not the matter) as he hath done
exactly : For Plato ever writ these high
matters in easy and familiar dialogues ;
and made the philosophers, and learned
men of that age ; as Simias, Cebes,
Timæus, Callias, Phædon, &c, yea and
Socrates himself, the Interlocutors ; although they never heard any thing of it
till the book came out : And as talking
of State-Affairs in a Monarchy must
needs be more offensive, than it was in
the Democracy where Plato lived ; therefore our author has forborn the naming
the persons who constitute this dialogue :
Yet he does make a pretty near representation and character of some persons,
who (I dare swear) never heard of this
discourse, nor of the author's design
This convinced me, and made me suffer
the title to pass. So that I have nothing more to say to thee, courteous
reader, but to desire thee to pardon the
faults in printing ; and also the plain-
ness and easiness of the stile, and some
tautologies : which latter I could easily
have

have mended, but that I thought the author did not let them pass out of neglect, but design; and intended that both they, and the familiarity of the words and expressions, suited better with his purpose of disposing this matter to be treated in ordinary conversation amongst private friends, than full periods and starch'd language would have done; which might have been impropriety. The next request I have to thee is: that if thou dost believe this discourse to be a very foolish one, as it may be for aught I know, (for I am no fit judge of such matters) that thou wilt yet vouchsafe to suspend thy censure of it for a while, till the whole impression is vended; that so, although neither the publick nor thyself may ever reap any benefit or profit by it, I may be yet so fortunate by thy favour as to do it: Which will make me study thy content hereafter in something better, and in the mean time remain,

Thy Friend and Servant.

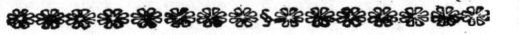

PLATO *Redivivus:*

OR,

DIALOGUES

Concerning

GOVERNMENT.

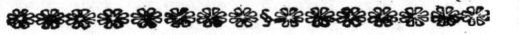

✿✿✿✿✿✿✿✿✿✿✿§✿✿✿✿✿✿✿✿✿✿✿

The ARGUMENT.

*A Noble Venetian, (not one of the young
fry, but a. grave sober person who had
born office and magistracy in his own
commonwealth,) having been some years
since in France, with a near relation of
his who was ambassadour at that court,
and finding himself out of employment ;
resolved to divert himself, by visiting
some part of the world which he had
never seen : and so passing thro' Germany, Flanders, and Holland, arrived
in England, about the beginning of May
last ; bringing letters of recommendation
to several English gentlemen, who had
been travellers, and made friendship in
his country : a custom, usually practised
amongst such who travel into any part,
where they have no habitude or acquaintance. Amongst the rest, he was addressed to one of the gentlemen who acts
a part in this dialogue. Who, after he
had*

had waited upon him and served him
for near two months, had certain necessary occasions, which called him for
some time into the country : where he
had not been above three weeks, before
he heard, by meer accident, that the
gentleman of Venice was fallen dangerous sick of a malignant fever : which
made him post away immediately to London, to assist and serve him in what he
might. But he found him almost perfectly restored to his health, by an
eminent physician of our nation ; as renowned for his skill and cures at home,
as for his writings both here and abroad :
and who (besides his profound knowledge
in all learning as well in other pro-
fessions as his own) had particularly
arriv'd to so exact and perfect a discovery of the formerly hidden parts of
human bodies ; that every one, who can
but understand Latin, may by his means
know more of anatomy, than either
Hippocrates, or any of the ancients or
moderns, did or do perceive : and if he
had lived in the days of Solomon, that
great philosopher would never have said,

cor hominis inscrutabile. *This excellent doctor being in the sick man's chamber, when the other English gentleman newly alighted, came to visit him; after some compliments and conversation of course, they begun to talk of political matters: as you will better understand, by the introduction and by the discourse itself.*

PLATO

PLATO *Redivivus:*

OR,

DIALOGUES

Concerning

GOVERNMENT.

The First DIALOGUE.

English Gentleman.

THE sudden news I had of your sad distemper, and the danger you were in, has been the cause of a great deal of affliction to me; as well as of my present and speedy repair to London, some week^s sooner than I intended. I must confess I received some comfort to hear at my arri-

B 3   rival

rival of your amendment ; and do take much more now to find you up, and as I hope recover'd : which I knew would be a neceffary confequence of your fending for this excellent phyfician, the Efculapius of our age ; it being the firft requeft I had to make to you, if by feeing him here in your chamber I had not found it needlefs. For the deftiny of us Englifhmen depends upon him ; and we either live or die infallibly, according to the judgment or good fortune we have when we are fick, either to call or not call him to our affiftance.

Noble Venetian. I am infinitely obliged to you, for your care of me ; but am forry it has been fo inconvenient to you, as to make you leave your affairs in the country fooner than you propofed to yourfelf to do. I wifh I might be fo fortunate in the courfe of my life, as to find an opportunity of making fome part of an acknowledgment, for this and all the reft of your favours ; but fhall pray God it may not be in the fame kind : but that your health may ever be fo entire, that you never need fo tranfcendent a charity, as I now receive from your goodnefs. And as to this incomparable doctor ;

                                        although,

although, I muſt confeſs, that all the good which has happen'd to me in this country, as well as the knowledge I have received of perſons and things, does derive from you; yet I muſt make an exception, as to this one point : for if I can either read or hear, this gentleman's excellent writings, and the fame he worthily enjoys in my country, would have made it inexcuſable in me to implore the help of any other. And I do aſſure you, that, before I left England, it was in my ambition to beg your mediation towards the bringing me into the acquaintance and favour of this learned perſon ; even before I had any thoughts of becoming the object of his care and ſkill, as now I am the trophy of both.

Doctor. Well, gentlemen, you are both too great to be flatterers, and I too little to be flattered ; and therefore I will impute this fine diſcourſe you both make about me, to the overflowing of your wit, and the having no object near you to vent it upon but me. And for you, ſir, if my art fail me not, the voiding this mirth is a very good ſign that you are in a fair way to a perfect recovery. And for my countryman here,

here, I hope whilſt he has this vent, that his hypochondriack diſtemper will be at quiet; and that neither his own thoughts, nor the ill poſture of our publick affairs, will make him hang himſelf, for at leaſt this twelve-month.   Only, gentlemen, pray take notice, that this does not paſs upon me, nor do I drink it like milk (as the French phraſe it ;) being mindful of what a grave gentleman at Florence replyed to a young eſquire, (who anſwered his compliments with, " Oh, ſir, you flatter me, ") *I prencipi s'adulano, i pari voſtri ſi coglionono.* That laſt word I cannot render well into Latin.

Engliſh Gentleman. Well, doctor, we will not offend your modeſty : the next time we do you juſtice, it ſhall be behind your back, ſince you are ſo ſevere upon us. But you may aſſure yourſelf, that my intention of recommending you to this gentleman, was for his own ſake and not for yours : for you have too many patients already ; and it were much better, both for you and us, that you had but half ſo many : for then we ſhould have more of your writings, and ſometimes

enjoy

enjoy your good converfation; which is worth our being fick on purpofe for: and I am refolved to put my felf fometimes into my bed, and fend for you, fince you have done coming to our coffee-houfe.

But to leave this fubject now; I hear you fay, that this gentleman is in a perfect way of recovery: pray is he well enough to hear, without any prejudice to his convalefcence, a reprehenfion I have to make him?

Doct. Yes, yes, you may fay what you will to him; for your reprimands will rather divert than trouble him, and prove more a cordial than a corrofive.

Eng. Gent. Then, fir, pray confider what fatisfaction you can ever make me for the hard meafure you have ufed towards me, in letting me learn from common fame and fortune, the news of your ficknefs, and that not till your recovery; and for depriving me of the opportunity of paying the debt I owe to your own merit, and to the recommendation of thofe worthy perfons in Italy, who did me the honour to addrefs you to me. And this injury is much aggravated by the fplen-

B 5

dour of your condition, and greatness of your fortune ; which makes it impossible for me ever to hope for any other occasion to express my faithful service to you, or satisfie any part of the duty I have to be at your devotion. To be sick in a strange country, and to distrust the sincerity and obedience of——

Noble Ven. Pray, sir, give me leave to interrupt you, and to assure you, that it was not any distrust of your goodness to me, of which I have had sufficient experience ; nor any insensibleness how much your care might advantage me ; much less any scruple I had of being more in your debt ; which if it had been possible for me to entertain, it must have been thought of long since, before I had received those great obligations, which I never made any difficulty to accept of. It was not, I say, any of these considerations, which hinder'd me from advertising you of my distemper ; but the condition and nature of it, which in a moment depriv'd me of the exercise of those faculties which might give me a capacity of helping myself in any thing. But

But otherwife I affure you that no day of my life fhall pafs, wherein I will not exprefs a fenfe of your favours ; and------

Doct. Pray now, fir, permit me to interrupt you ; for this gentleman, I dare fay, looks for no compliments : but that which I have to fay, is ; that the defire you fignified to me, to give you fome account of our affairs here, and the turbulency of our prefent ftate, will be much better placed, if you pleafe to addrefs it to this gentleman, whofe parts and ftudies have fitted him for fuch an employment ; befides his having had a great fhare in the managing affairs of ftate here, in other times : and really no man underftands the government of England better than he.

Eng. Gent. Now, doctor, I fhould tell you, *i pari miei fi coglionono* ; for fo you yourfelf have baptized this kind of civility. But however, this is a province that I cannot be reafonably preft to take upon me, whilft you are prefent ; who are very well known to be as fkillful in the nature and diftemper of the body politick,

litick, as the whole nation confesses you
to be in the concerns of the natural.
And you would have good store of practice in your former capacity, if the wise
custom amongst the ancient Greeks were
not totally out of use. For they, when
they found any craziness or indisposition
in their several governments, before it broke
out into a disease, did repair to the physicians of state (who, from their profession, were called the seven wise men of
Greece ;) and obtain'd from them some
good Recipes, to prevent those seeds of
distemper from taking root, and destroy-
ing the publick peace. But in our days, these
signs or forerunners of diseases in state
are not foreseen, till the whole mass is
corrupted ; and that the patient is incurable, but by violent remedies. And if
we could have perceived the first symp-
toms of our distemper, and used good al-
teratives, the curiosity of this worthy gentleman had been spared, as also his command to you to give him some light into our matters ; and we unfortunate Englishmen had reposed in that quiet, ease,
and security, which we enjoy'd three hundred

red years since. But let us leave the contest who shall inform this gentleman, lest
we spend the time we should do it in
unprofitably, and let each of us take his
part; for if one speak all, it will look like
a studied discourse fitted for the press, and
not a farmiliar dialogue. For it ought
to be in private conversation, as it was
originally in the planting the gospel; when
there were two sorts of preaching: the
one concionary, which was used by the
apostles and other missionaries, when they
spoke to those who had never heard of the
mysteries of Christian religion; possibly not
so much, as of the Jewish law or the
history of Christ; the duty of those was
to hear, and not reply, or any way interrupt the harangue: but when the believers
(called the church) assembled together,
it was the custom of such of the auditors
to whom any thing occurred, or (as saint
Paul calls it) was revealed, to interpose
and desire to be heard; which was called
an interlocutory preaching, or religious
conversation: and served very much to the
instructing and edifying those who had long
believed in Christ, and possibly knew as
much

much of him as their paftor himfelf; and
this is ufed ftill amongft many of our in-
dependent congregations.

Doct. I have (befides the reafon I alledged before, and which I ftill infift upon) fome other caufe to beg that you
will pleafe to give yourfelf the trouble of
anfwering this gentleman's queries; which
is, that I am very defective in my ex-
preffions in the Italian language : which
though I underftand perfectly, and fo comprehend all that either of you deliver; yet
I find not words at hand to fignifie my
own meaning, and am therefore neceffitated to deliver my felf in Latin, as you
fee. And I fear that our pronunciation
being fo different from that which is ufed
in Italy, this worthy perfon may not fo
eafily comprehend what I intend, and fo
be difappointed in the defire he hath to
be perfectly inftructed in our affairs.

Noble Ven. Really, fir, that is not all;
for befides that, I confefs your pronunciation of the Latin tongue to be very
new to me, and for that reafon I have
been forced to be troublefome to you, in
making you repeat things twice, or thrice.
                                    I fay

I say besides that, your Latinity, (as your writings shew and all the world knows) is very pure and elegant : which it is notorious to all, that we in Italy scarce understand ; gentlemen there never learning more Latin, than what is neceffary to call for meat and drink, in Germany or Holland, where most of the hosts speak a certain Franck, compounded of Dutch, Latin, and Italian. And though some of us have Latin enough to understand a good. author, (as you have of our language) yet we feldom arrive to speak any better than this Franck ; or can without study comprehend good Latin, when we meet with it in difcourfe. And therefore it is your perfection in that tongue, and my ignorance in it, that makes me concur with you, in defiring this gentleman to take the pains of inftructing my curiofity in Italian.

Eng. Gent. I fhall obey you in this, and all things elfe, upon this condition, that both you and the doctor will vouchfafe to interrogate me, and by that means give me the method of ferving you in this : and then that you will both pleafe to interrupt

terrupt and contradict me, when you think I say any thing amiss, or that either of you are of a different opinion ; and to give me a good occasion of explaining my self, and possibly of being convinced by you, which I shall easily confess ; for I hate nothing more than to hear disputes amongst gentlemen and men of sense, wherein the speakers seem (like sophisters in a college) to dispute rather for victory, than to discover and find out the truth.

Doct. Well, all this I believe will be granted you ; so that we have nothing to do now, but to adjourn, and name a time when to meet again. Which I, being this gentleman's physician, will take upon me to appoint : and it shall be to-morrow morning about nine of the clock, after he has slept well ; as I hope he will, by means of a cordial I intend to send him immediately. In the mean time, not to weary him too much, we will take our leaves of him for this night.

Noble Ven. I shall expect your return with great impatience ; and if your cordial be not very potent, I believe the desire of seeing you will make me wake

much

much fooner than the hour you appoint : and I am very confident, that my mind as well as my body, will be fufficiently improved by fuch vifits. It begins to be darkifh ; boy, light your torch, and wait on thefe gentlemen down.

Both. Sir, we wifh you all good reft and health.

Noble Ven. And I, with a thoufand thanks, the like to you.

The

✿✿✿✿✿✿✿✿✿✿✿✿:✿✿✿✿✿✿✿✿✿✿✿✿✿

The Second DIALOGUE.

Doct. WELL, sir, how is it? have you rested well to night? I fear we come too early.

Noble Ven. Dear doctor, I find myself very well, thanks to your care and skill; and have been up above these two hours, in expectation of the favour you and this gentleman promis'd me.

Doct. Well, then pray let us leave off compliments and repartees (of which we had a great deal too much yesterday) and fall to our business; and be pleas'd to interrogate this gentleman what you think fit.

Noble Ven. Then, sir, my first request to you is, that you will vouchsafe to acquaint me for what reasons this nation, which hath ever been esteemed (and very justly) one of the most considerable people of the world; and made the best figure both in peace, treaties, war, and trade; is now of so small regard, and signifies so little abroad? Pardon the freedom I take, for I assure you it is not

out

out of difrespect, much less of contempt that
I speak it : for since I arriv'd in England, I
find it one of the most flourishing kingdoms
in Europe, full of splendid nobility and gentry ; the comliest persons alive, valiant, courteous, knowing, and bountiful ; and as
well stored with commoners, honest, indus-
trious, fitted for business, merchandise, arts,
or arms ; as their several educations lead
them. Those who apply themselves to study, prodigious for learning, and succeeding
to admiration in the perfection of all sciences :
all this makes the riddle impossible to be
solved ; but by some skillful OEdipus, such
as you are ; whose pains I will yet so far
spare, as to acknowledge, that I do in that
little time I have spent here, perceive that
the immediate cause of all this, is the dif-
union of the people and the governors ; the
discontentment of the gentry, and turbulency of the commonalty ; although without all violence or tumult, which is mira-
culous. So that what I now request of you,
is, that you will please to deduce particularly to me, the causes of this division ; that
when they are laid open, I may proceed (if
you think fit to permit it) from the disease
when

when known, to enquire after the remedies.

Eng. Gent. Before I come to make you
any answer, I muſt thank you for the worthy and honourable character you give of our
nation; and ſhall add to it, that I do verily
believe, that there are not a more loyal and
faithful people to their prince in the whole
world, than ours are; nor that fear more to
fall into that ſtate of confuſion, in which
we were twenty years ſince : and that, not
only this parliament, which conſiſts of the
moſt eminent men of the kingdom, both
for eſtates and parts; but all the inhabitants
of this iſle in general; even thoſe (ſo many
of them as have their underſtandings yet
entire) which were of the anti-royal party
in our late troubles, have all of them the
greateſt horror imaginable to think of doing any thing, that may bring this poor
country into thoſe dangers and uncertainties,
which then did threaten our ruin. And the
rather for this conſideration : that neither
the wiſdom of ſome who were engaged in
thoſe affairs, which I muſt aver to have been
very great; nor the ſucceſs of their conteſt,
which ended in an abſolute victory; could
prevail

prevail fo, as to give this kingdom any advantage; nay not fo much as any settlement, in fatisfaction and requital of all the blood it had loft, money it had fpent, and hazard it had run. A clear argument why we muft totally exclude a civil war from being any of the remedies, when we come to that point. I muft add farther; that as we have as loyal fubjects as are any where to be found, fo we have as gracious and good a prince : I never having yet heard that he did or attempted to do, any the leaft act of arbitrary power, in any publick concern ; nor did ever take, or endeavour to take from any particular perfon the benefit of the law. And for his only brother, (altho' accidentally he cannot be denied to be a great motive of the people's unquietnefs,) all men muft acknowledge him to be a moft glorious and honourable prince : one who has expofed his life feveral times for the fafety and glory of this nation ; one who pays juftly and punctually his debts, and manages his own fortune difcreetly, and yet keeps the beft court and equipage of any fubject in Chriftendom ; is courteous and affable to all ; and in fine, has nothing in

his

his whole conduct to be excepted against,
much less dreaded ; excepting, that he is
believed to be of a religion contrary to the
honour of God, and the safety and interest
of this people, which gives them just ap-
prehensions of their future condition. But
of this matter we shall have occasion to spe-
culate hereafter ; in the mean time, since
we have such a prince, and such subjects,
we must needs want the ordinary cause of
distrust and division ; and therefore must
seek higher, to find out the original of this
turbulent posture we are in.

Doct. Truly, you had need seek higher,
or lower, to satisfy us ; for hitherto, you
have but enforced the gentleman's question,
and made us more admire what the solution
will be.

Eng. Gent. Gentlemen, then I shall delay you no longer. The evil counsellors,
the pensioner-parliament, the thorow-pac'd
judges, the flattering divines, the busy and
designing papists, the French counsels, are
not the cause of our misfortunes ; they are
but the effects, (as our present distractions
are) of one primary cause ; which is, the
breach and ruin of our government : which,
having

having been decaying for near two hundred
years, is in our age brought so near to ex-
piration, that it lies agonizing ; and can no
longer perform the functions of a political
life ; nor carry on the work of ordering and
preserving mankind. So that the shifts that
our courtiers have within some years used,
are but so many tricks, or conclusions which
they are trying, to hold life and soul together a while longer : and, have played
handy-dandy with parliaments, (and especially with the house of commons, the only
part which is now left entire of the old constitution) by adjourning, and proroguing,
and diffolving them ; contrary to the true
meaning of the law ; as well in the reign
of our late king, as during his majesty's
that now is. Whereas indeed our counsellors (perceiving the decay of the foundation, as they must if they can see but one
inch into the politicks) ought to have address'd themselves to the king to call a parliament, the true physician, and to lay open
the distemper there ; and so have endeavoured a cure, before it had been too late : as
I fear, it now is ; I mean, for the piecing
and patching up the old government. It is
true,

I

true, as the divine Machiavil fays, that difeafes in government are like a marafmus in
the body natural, which is very hard to be
difcovered, whilft it is curable; and after
it comes to be eafy to difcern, difficult (if
not impoffible) to be remedy'd: yet it is to
be fuppofed that the counfellors are, or
ought to be fkillful phyficians; and to forefee the feeds of ftate-diftempers, time
enough to prevent the death of the patient:
elfe they ought in confcience to excufe themfelves from that fublime employment, and
betake themfelves to callings more fuitable
to their capacities. So that although for
this reafon, the minifters of ftate here are
inexcufable; and deferve all the fury, which
muft one time or other be let loofe againft
them; (except they fhall fuddenly fly from
the wrath to come, by finding out in time
and advifing the true means of fetting themfelves to rights:) yet neither prince nor people are in the mean time to be blamed, for
not being able to conduct things better;
no more, than the waggoner is to anfwer
for his ill guiding, or the oxen for their ill
drawing the waggon; when it is with age
and ill ufage broken, and the wheels unfer-
viceable;

viceable; or the pilot and mariners, for not weathering out a storm; when the ship hath sprung a plank. And as in the body of man, sometimes the head and all the members are in good order, nay, the vital parts are sound and entire; yet if there be a considerable putrification in the humours, much more, if the blood (which the scripture calls the life) be impure and corrupted; the patient ceases not to be in great danger, and oftentimes dies without some skilful physician: and in the mean time the head and all the parts suffer, and are unquiet, full as much, as if they were all immediately affected: so it is in every respect with the body politick, or commonwealth, when their foundations are moulder'd. And although in both these cases, the patients cannot (though the distemper be in their own bodies) know what they ail, but are forced to send for some artist to tell them; yet they cease not to be extreamly uneasy and impatient, and lay hold oftentimes upon unsuitable remedies, and impute their malady to wrong and ridiculous causes. As some people do here, who think that the growth of popery is our only evil; and that if we

C   were

were secure against that, our peace and settlement were obtain'd; and that our disease needed no other cure. But of this more when we come to the cure.

Noble Ven. Against this discourse, certainly we have nothing to reply : but must grant, that when any government is decay'd, it must be mended; or all will ruin. But now we must request you to declare to us, how the government of England is decay'd; and how it comes to be so. For I am one of those unskilful persons that cannot discern a state-marasmus, when the danger is so far off.

Eng. Gent. Then no man living can; for your government is this day the only school in the world, that breeds such physicians, and you are esteemed one of the ablest amongst them : and it would be manifest to all the world for truth, altho' there were no argument for it, but the admirable stability and durableness of your government; which hath lasted above twelve hundred years entire and perfect. Whereas all the rest of the countries in Europe, have not only changed masters very frequently in a quarter of that time; but have varied and altered their

3.

their polities very often. Which manifests
that you must needs have ever enjoy'd a
succeffion of wife citizens, that have had
fkill and ability to forewarn you betimes of
thofe rocks againft which your excellently-
built veffel might in time fplit.

Noble Ven. Sir, you over-value, not only
me, but the wifdom of my fellow-citizens;
for we have none of thefe high fpeculations,
nor hath fcarce any of our body read
Ariftotle, Plato, or Cicero, or any of thofe
great artifts ancient or modern, who teach
that great fcience of the governing and in-
creafing great ftates and cities: without
ftudying which fcience no man can be fit to
difcourfe pertinently of thefe matters; much
lefs to found, or mend a government, or
fo much as find the defects of it. We only
ftudy our own government; and that too
chiefly to be fit for advantagious employments, rather than to forefee our dangers.
Which yet, I muft needs confefs, fome
amongft us are pretty good at; and will in
a harangue, made upon paffing a law, venture to tell us what will be the confequence
of it two hundred years hence. But of
thefe things I fhall be very prodigal in my

difcourfe,

difcourfe, when you have leifure and patience to command me to fay any thing of
our polity; in the mean time pray be pleafed
to go on with your edifying inftruction.

Eng. Gent. Before I can tell you how the
government of England came to be decay'd,
I muft tell you what that government was;
and what it now is. And I fhould fay fomething too of government in general, but
that I am afraid of talking of that fubject
before you who are fo exact a judge of it.

Noble Ven. I thought you had been pleafed
to have done with this difcourfe. I affure
you, fir, if I had more fkill in that matter
than ever I can pretend to, it would but
ferve to make me the fitter auditor of what
you fhall fay on that fubject.

Eng. Gent. Sir, in the courfe of my reafoning upon this point, I fhall have occafion to infift and expatiate upon many
things, which both myfelf and others have
publifh'd in former times. For which I
will only make this excufe; that the repetition of fuch matters is the more par-
donable, becaufe they will be at leaft new
to you who are a ftranger to our affairs
and writings. And the rather, becaufe thofe

difcourfes

difcourfes fhall be apply'd to our prefent
condition, and fuited to our prefent occafions. But I will fay no more ; but obey
you, and proceed. I will not take upon me
to fay, or fo much as conjecture, how and
when government began in the world ; or
what government is moft ancient. Hiftory
muft needs be filent in that point : for that
government is more ancient than hiftory ;
and there was never any writer but was bred
under fome government ; which is neceffarily fuppofed to be the parent of all arts
and fciences, and to have produced them.
And therefore it would be as hard for a
man to write an account of the beginning
of the laws and polity of any country, except there were memory of it ; (which cannot be before the firft hiftoriographer :)
as it would be to any perfon, without records, to tell the particular hiftory of his
own birth.

Doct. Sir, I cannot comprehend you :
may not hiftorians write a hiftory of matters
done before they were born ? If it were
fo, no man could write but of his own
times.

Eng.

Eng. Gent. My meaning is, where there are not ſtories, or records, extant; for as for oral tradition, it laſts but for one age, and then degenerates into fable : I call any thing in writing, whereby the account of the paſſages or occurrences of former times is derived to our knowledge, a hiſtory ; although it be not pen'd methodically, ſo as to make the author paſs for a wit : and had rather read the authentick records of any country, that is a collection of their laws and letters concerning tranſactions of ſtate and the like, than the moſt eloquent and judicious narrative that can be made.

Noble Ven. Methinks, ſir, your diſcourſe ſeems to imply, that we have no account extant of the beginning of governments. Pray what do you think of the books of Moſes ? Which ſeem to be pen'd on purpoſe to inform us how he, by God's command, led that people out of Egypt into another land ; and in the way made them a government. Beſides, does not Plutarch tell us, how Theſeus gathered together the diſperſed inhabitants of Attica, brought them into one city, and under one government of his own making ? The like did Romulus in Italy,

Italy, and many others in divers countries.

Eng. Gent. I never faid, that we had not fufficient knowledge of the original of particular governments; but it is evident, that thefe great legiflators had feen and lived under other adminiftrations, and had the help of learned law-givers and philofophers; excepting the firft, who had the aid of God himfelf. So that it remains undifcovered yet, how the firft regulation of mankind began: and therefore I will take for granted that which all the politicians conclude: which is, that neceffity made the firft government. For every man by the firft law of nature (which is common to us and brutes) had, like beafts in a pafture, right to every thing; and there being no property, each individual, if he were the ftronger, might feize whatever any other had poffeffed himfelf of before, which made a ftate of perpetual war. To remedy which, and the fear that nothing fhould be long enjoy'd by any particular perfon, (neither was any man's life in fafety,) every man confented to be debarr'd of that univerfal right to all things; and confine himfelf to a quiet

and

and secure enjoyment of such a part, as should be allotted him. Thence came in ownership, or property : to maintain which, it was necessary to consent to laws, and a government ; to put them in execution. Which of the governments now extant, or that have been formerly, was first, is not possible now to be known : but I think this must be taken for granted, that whatsoever the frame or constitution was first, it was made by the persuasion and mediation of some wise and vertuous person, and consented to by the whole number. And then, that it was instituted for the good and preservation of the governed; and not for the exaltation and greatness of the person or persons appointed to govern. The reason why I beg this concession is, that it seems very improbable, not to say impossible, that a vast number of people should ever be brought to consent to put themselves under the power of others, but for the ends abovesaid, and so lose their liberty without advantaging themselves in any thing. And it is full as impossible that any person (or persons so inconsiderable in number as magistrates and rulers are) should by force

get

get an empire to themselves. Though I am not ignorant that a whole people have in imminent dangers, either from the invasion of a powerful enemy, or from civil diftractions, put themfelves wholly into the hands of one illuftrious perfon for a time; and that with good fuccefs, under the beft forms of government: but this is nothing to the original of ftates.

Noble Ven. Sir, I wonder how you come to pafs over the confideration of paternal government, which is held to have been the beginning of monarchies.

Eng. Gen. Really, I did not think it worth the taking notice of: for though it be not eafy to prove a negative, yet I believe if we could trace all foundations of polities that now are, or ever came to our knowledge fince the world began; we fhall find none of them to have defcended from paternal power. We know nothing of Adam's leaving the empire to Cain, or Seth: it was impoffible for Noah to retain any jurifdiction over his own three fons; who were difperfed into three parts of the world, if our antiquaries calculate right: and as for Abraham, whilft he lived, as alfo his fon

C 5

Ifaac,

Ifaac, they were but ordinary fathers of families, and no queftion governed their own
houfhold as all others do. And when Ja-
cob upon his death-bed did relate to his
children the promife almighty God had made
his grandfather ; to make him a great nation, and give his pofterity a fruitful territory ; he fpeaks not one word of the empire of Reuben his firft-born, but fuppofes
them all equal. And fo they were taken
to be by Mofes, when he divided the land
to them by lot ; and by God's command
made them a commonwealth. So that I
believe this fancy to have been firft ftarted,
not by the folid judgment of any man, but
to flatter fome prince ; and to affert, for
want of better arguments, the *jus divinum*
of monarchy.

Noble Ven. I have been impertinent in
interrupting you, but yet now I cannot
repent of it, fince your anfwer hath given
me fo much fatisfaction ; but if it be fo as
you fay, that government was at firft inftituted for the intereft and prefervation of
mankind, how comes it pafs, that there are
and have been fo many abfolute monarchies
in the world, in which it feems that nothing
is

is provided for, but the greatnefs and power of the prince?

Eng. Gent. I have prefumed to give you already my reafon, why I take for granted, that fuch a power could never be given by the confent of any people, for a perpetuity: for though the people of Ifrael did againft the will of Samuel, and indeed of God himfelf, demand and afterwards chufe them-felves a king; yet he was never fuch a king as we fpeak of; for that all the orders of their commonwealth, the fanhedrim, the congregation of the people, the princes of the tribes, &c. did ftill remain in being: as hath been excellently proved by a learned gentleman of our nation, to whom I refer you. It may then be enquired into, how thefe monarchies at firft did arife. Hiftory being in this point filent as to the ancient principalities, we will conjecture, that fome of them might very well proceed from the corruption of better governments, which muft neceffarily caufe a depravation in manners; (as nothing is more certain than that politick defects breed moral ones, as our nation is a pregnant example) this debauchery of man-ners might blind the underftandings of a

C 6   great

great many; deftroy the fortunes of others, and make them indigent; infufe into very many a neglect and carelefnefs of the publick good (which in all fettled ftates is very much regarded) fo that it might eafily come into the ambition of fome bold afpiring perfon, to affect empire; and as eafily into his power, (by fair pretences with fome, and promifes of advantages with others,) to procure followers, and gain a numerous party, either to ufurp tyranny over his own country, or to lead men forth to conquer and fubdue another. Thus it is fuppofed that Nimrod got his kingdom: who in fcripture is called, a great hunter before God; which expofitors interpret, a great tyrant. The modern defpotical powers have been acquired by one of thefe two ways. Either by pretending, by the firft founder thereof, that he had a divine miffion; and fo gaining not only followers, but even eafy accefs in fome places without force, to empire, and afterwards dilating their power by great conquefts; thus Mahomet and Cingis Can began, and eftablifhed the Saracen and Tartarian kingdoms: or by a long feries of wifdom in a prince, or chief magiftrate of

a

a mixt monarchy, and his council, who by reason of the sleepiness and inadvertency of the people, have been able to extinguish the great nobility, or render them inconfiderable; and so by degrees taking away from the people their protectors, render them flaves. So the monarchies of France, and some other countries, have grown to what they are at this day; there being left but a shadow of the three ftates in any of thefe monarchies, and so no bounds remaining to the regal power. But fince property remains ftill to the fubjects; thefe governments may be faid to be changed, but not founded or eftablifhed: for there is no maxim more infallible and holding in any fcience, than this is in politicks; that empire is founded in property. Force or fraud may alter a goverment; but it is property that muft found and eternife it. Upon this undeniable aphorifm we are to build moft of our fubfequent reafoning: in the mean time we may fuppofe, that hereafter the great power of the king of France may diminifh much, when his enraged and opprefled fubjects come to be commanded by a prince of lefs courage, wifdom, and military

litary virtue; when it will be very hard
for any such king to govern tyrannically a
country, which is not entirely his own.

Doct. Pray, sir, give me leave to ask
you by the way, what is the reason that
here in our country where the peerage is
lessened sufficiently, the king has not gotten as great an addition of power as accrues
to the crown of France?

Eng. Gent. You will understand that,
doctor, before I have finish'd this discourse:
but to stay your stomach till then, you may
please to know that in France the greatness of the nobility which has been lately
taken from them, did not consist in vast
riches and revenues; but in great privileges, and jurisdictions, which obliged the
people to obey them: whereas our great
peers in former times had not only the same
great dependences, but very considerable
revenues besides, in demesnes, and otherwise. This vassalage over the people, which
the peers of France had, being abolish'd, the
power over those tenants, which before was
in their lords, fell naturally and of course into
the crown; although the lands and possef-
sions divested of those dependences did and

do

do ftill remain to the owners : whereas here in England, though the fervices are for the moft part worn out, and infignificant ; yet for want of providence and policy in former kings, who could not forfee the danger a-far off, entails have been fuffered to be cut off ; and fo two parts in ten of all thofe vaft eftates, as well manors as demefnes, by the luxury and folly of the owners, have been within thefe two hundred years purchafed by the lefTer gentry and the commons ; which has been fo far from advantaging the crown, that it has made the country fcarce governable by monarchy. But if you pleafe, I will go on with my difcourfe about government, and come to this again hereafter.

Noble Ven. I befeech you, fir, do.

Eng. Gen. I cannot find by the fmall reading I have, that there were any other governments in the world anciently than thefe three ; Monarchy, Ariftocracy, and Democracy. For the firft ; I have no light out of antiquity to convince me, that there were in old times any other monarchies, but fuch as were abfolutely defpotical. All kingdoms then, as well in Greece, (Macedon,

don, Epirus, and the like, where it is said the princes exercised their power moderately) as in Asia, being altogether unlimited by any laws, or any assemblies of nobility or people. Yet I must confess, Aristotle, when he reckons up the corruptions of these three governments, calls tyranny the corruption of monarchy : by which if he means a change of government, (as it is in the corruptions of the other two ;) then it must follow, that the philosopher knew of some other monarchy at the first, which afterwards degenerated into tyranny ; that is, into arbitrary power : (for so the word tyranny is most commonly taken, though in modern languages it signifies the ill exercise of power ;) for certainly arbitrary government cannot be called tyranny, where the whole property is in the prince, (as we reasonably suppose it to have been in those monarchies ;) no more than it is tyranny for you to govern your own house and estate as you please. But it is possible Aristotle might not in this speak so according to terms of art, but might mean, that the ill government of a kingdom or family is tyranny. However we have one example, that

puzzles.

puzzles politicians: and that is Egypt, where
Pharaoh is called king; and yet we see, that
till Joseph's time he had not the whole property: for the wisdom of that patriarch
taught his master a way to make a new
use of that famine, by telling him, that if
they would buy their lives, and sell their
estates (as they did afterwards, and preserve
themselves by the king's bread) they shall
serve Pharaoh: which shews that Joseph
knew well, that empire was founded in
property. But most of the modern writers
in polity, are of opinion, that Egypt was
not a monarchy till then; though the prince
might have the title of king: as the Hera-
clides had in Sparta, and Romulus and the
other kings had in Rome; both which
states were instituted commonwealths. They
give good conjectures for this their opinion,
too many to be here mentioned; only one
is, that originally (as they go about to
prove) all arts and sciences had their rise in
Egypt; which they think very improbable
to have been under a monarchy. But this
position, that all kings in former times
were absolute, is not so essential to the intent I have in this discourse; which is to
prove,

prove, that in all states, of what kind foever, this aphorifm takes place : *Imperium
fundatur in dominio.* So that if there were
mixed monarchies, then the king had not
all the property ; but thofe who fhared with
him in the adminiftration of the foveraignty, had their part (whether it were the fenate, the people, or both) or if he had no
companions in the foveraign power, he had
no fharers likewife in the dominion or poffeffion of the land. For that is all we mean
by property, in all this difcourfe ; for as
for perfonal eftate, the fubjects may enjoy
it in the largeft proportion, without being
able to invade the empire : the prince may
when he pleafes take away their goods by
his tenants and vaffals, (without an army ;)
which are his ordinary force, and anfwers
to our *poffe comitatus* ; but the fubjects with
their money cannot invade his crown. So
that all the defcription we need make of
this kind or form of government, is, that
the whole poffeffion of the country, and
the whole power lies in the hands and
breaft of one man ; he can make laws,
break and repeal them when he pleafes, or
difpenfe with them in the mean time when
he

he thinks fit ; interpose in all judicatories,
in behalf of his favourites ; take away any
particular man's perſonal eſtate, and his life
too, without the formality of a criminal
proceſs, or trial ; ſend a dagger, or a halter
to his chief miniſters, and command them
to make themſelves away ; and in fine, do
all that his will, or his intereſt, ſuggeſts to
him.

Doct. You have dwelt long here upon
an argumentation, that the ancients had
no monarchies but what were arbitrary——

Eng. Gent. Pray give me leave to ſave
your objections to that point, and to aſſure
you firſt ; that I will not take upon me to
be ſo poſitive in that ; for that I cannot pretend to have read all the hiſtorians and antiquaries that ever writ ; nor have I ſo perfect a memory as to remember, or make
uſe of, in a verbal and tranſient reaſoning,
all that I have ever read : and then to aſſure you again, that I build nothing upon
that aſſertion ; and ſo your objection will
be needleſs, and only take up time.

Doct. You miſtake me ; I had no intent
to uſe any argument or example againſt
your opinion in that, but am very willing
to.

to believe that it may be fo. What I was
going to fay was this, that you have in-
fifted much upon the point of monarchy,
and made a ftrange defcription of it ; whereas many of the ancients, and almoft all the
modern writers, magnify it to be the beft
of governments.

Eng. Gent. I have faid nothing to the
contrary. I have told you *de facto,* what
it is ; which I believe none will deny. The
philofopher faid it was the beft government ;
but with this reftriction, *ubi philofophi reg-
nant :* and they had an example of it, in
fome few Roman emperors : but in the moft
turbulent times of the commonwealth,
and factions between the nobility and the
people, Rome was much more full of virtuous and heroick citizens, than ever it
was under Aurelius or Antoninus. For the
moderns that are of that judgment ; they
are moft of them divines, not politicians :
and fomething may be faid in their behalf,
when by their good preaching, they can infufe into their imaginary prince, (who feems
already to have an image of the power of
God,) the juftice, wifdom, and goodnefs
too of the Deity.

Noble

Noble Ven. We are well satisfied with the progress you have hitherto made in this matter. Pray go on to the two other forms used amongst the ancients, and their corruptions; that so we may come to the modern governments, and see how England stands; and how it came to decay, and what must rebuild it.

Eng. Gent. You have very good reason to hasten me to that; for indeed, all that has been said yet, is but as it were a preliminary discourse to the knowledge of the government of England, and its decay: when it comes to the cure, I hope you will both help me, for both yourself and the doctor are a thousand times better than I at remedies. But I shall dispatch the other two governments. Aristocracy, or Optimacy, is a commonwealth, where the better sort, (that is, the eminent and rich men,) have the chief administration of the government: I say, the chief; because there are very few ancient Optimacies, but the people had some share: as in Sparta, where they had power to vote, but not debate; for so the oracle of Apollo, brought by Lycurgus

from

from Delphos, settles it. But the truth is,
these people were the natural Spartans ; for
Lycurgus divided the country or territory of
Laconia into 39000 shares ; whereof nine
thousand only of these owners were inhabitants of Sparta ; the rest lived in the country : so that altho' Thucidides call it an
aristocracy, and so I follow him, yet it
was none of those aristocracies usually de-
scribed by the politicians ; where the lands
of the territory were in a great deal
fewer hands. But call it what you will,
where ever there was an aristocracy, there
the property, or very much the over-
ballance of it, was in the hands of the
Aristoi or governors ; be they more or
fewer : for if the people have the greatest interest in the property, they will,
and must have it in the empire. A notable example of it is Rome, the best
and most glorious government that ever
the sun saw ; where the lands being equally divided amongst the tribes (that is, the
people) it was impossible for the Patricii
to keep them quiet, till they yielded to
their desires : not only to have their Tri-
bunes, to see that nothing passed into a law
                                        without

without their confent, but alfo to have it declared, that both the Confuls fhould not only be chofen by the people (as they ever were, and the Kings too before them) but that they might be elected too, when the people pleafed, out of Plebeian families. So that now I am come to Democracy. Which you fee is a government where the chief part of the foveraign power, and the exercife of it, refides in the People; and where the ftile is *Juffu populi, authoritate patrum.* And it doth confift of three fundamental orders; the fenate propofing, the people refolving, and the magiftrates executing. This government is much more powerful than Ariftocracy; becaufe the latter cannot arm the people, for fear they fhould feize upon the government; and therefore are fain to make ufe of none but ftrangers and mercenaries for foldiers: which, as the divine Machiavil fays, has hindred your commonwealth of Venice from mounting up to heaven; whither thofe incomparable orders, and that venerable wifdom ufed by your citizens in keeping to them, would have carried you; if in all your wars, you had not been ill ferved.

Doct.

Doct. Well, fir, pray let me afk you one thing concerning Venice: how do you make out your *Imperium fundatur in dominio* there? Have the gentlemen there, who are the party governing, the poffeffion of the whole territory? does not property remain entire to the gentlemen, and other inhabitants in the feveral countries of Padua, Brefcia, Vicenza, Verona, Bergamo, Creman, Trevifi, and Friuli; as alfo in the ultramarine provinces and iflands? And yet I believe you will not deny, but that the government of Venice is as well founded, and hath been of as long continuance, as any that now is or ever was in the world.

Eng. Gent. Doctor, I fhall not anfwer you in this; becaufe I am fure it will be better done by this gentleman, who is a worthy fon of that honourable mother.

Noble Ven. I thought you had faid, fir, that we fhould have done complimenting; but fince you do command me to clear the objection made by our learned doctor, I fhall prefume to tell you firft how our city began. The Goths, Huns, and

and Lombards coming with all the violence and cruelty imaginable to invade that part of Italy which we now call Terra firma, and where our anceſtors did then inhabit; forced them in great numbers to ſeek a ſhelter amongſt a great many little rocks, or iſlands, which ſtood very thick in a vaſt lake, or rather marſh, which is made by the Adriatique ſea; we call it Laguna: here they began to build, and getting boats, made themſelves proviſions of all kind from the land; from whence innumerable people began to come to them, finding that they could ſubſiſt, and that the barbarous people had no boats to attack them, nor that they could be invaded either by horſe or foot without them. Our firſt government, and which laſted for many years, was no more than what was practiſed in many country pariſhes in Italy, (and poſſibly here too,) where the clerk, or any other perſon, calls together the chief of the inhabitants to conſider of pariſh-buſineſs; as chuſing of officers, making of rates, and the like. So in Venice, when there was any publick proviſion to be made by way of law, or otherwiſe, ſome officers went about to perſons of the greateſt

D

wealth

wealth and credit, to intreat them to meet and
confult ; from whence our fenate is called to
this day *Configlio de pregadi*, which in our
barbarous idiom is as much as *Pregati* in Tuf-
can language. Our fecurity increafed daily ;
and fo by confequence our number and our
riches : for by this time there began to be a-
nother inundation of Sarazens upon Afia mi-
nor ; which forced a great many of the poor
people of Greece to fly to us for protection,
giving us the poffeffion of fome iflands, and
other places upon the continent. This o-
pened us a trade, and gave a beginning to
our greatnefs : but chiefly made us confider
what government was fitteft to conferve our
felves, and keep our wealth ; (for we did not
then much dream of conquefts, elfe without doubt we muft have made a popular government.) We pitcht upon an Ariftocracy : by ordering that thofe who had been
called to council for that prefent year and
for four years before, fhould have the government in their hands ; and all their pofterity after them for ever : which made firft
the diftinction between gentlemen and
citizens. The people, who confifted of divers nations, moft of them newly come to
                                    inhabit

inhabit there, and generally feeking nothing but fafety and eafe, willingly confented to this change; and fo this State hath continued to this day : though the feveral orders and councils have been brought in fince, by degrees; as our nobility encreafed, and for other caufes. Under this government we have made fome conquefts in Italy, and Greece : for our city ftood like a wall between the two great torrents of Goths and Sarazens; and as either of their empires declin'd, it was eafy for us, without being very warlike, to pick up fome pieces of each fide. As for the government of thefe conquefts : we did not think fit to divide the land among the nobility, for fear of envy, and the effects of it; much lefs did we think it advifeable to plant colonies of our people, which would have given the power into their hands; but we thought it the beft way for our government to leave the people their property, tax them what we thought fit, and keep them under by governours and citadels; and fo in fhort make them a province. So that now the doctor's riddle is folved; for I fuppofe this gentleman did not

D 2

mean

mean that his maxim fhould reach to provincial governments.

Eng. Gent. No, fir; fo far from that,
that it is juft contrary. For as in national or
domeftick government, where a nation is
governed either by its own people or its
own prince, there can be no fettled government, except they have the rule who poffefs the country : fo in provincial governments, if they be wifely ordered, no man
muft have any the leaft fhare in the managing affairs of ftate, but ftrangers ; or fuch
as have no fhare or part in the poffeffions
there ; for elfe they will have a very good
opportunity of fhaking off their yoke.

Doct. That is true ; and we are fo wife
here (I mean our anceftors were) as to have
made a law, that no native in Ireland can be
Deputy there. But, fir, being fully fatif-
fied in my demand by this gentleman, I befeech you to go on to what you have to fay
before you come to England.

Eng. Gent. I fhall then offer two things
to your obfervation ; the firft is, that in all
times and places, where any great heroes or
legiflators have founded a government, (by
gathering people together, to build a city,

or

or to invade any country to poſſeſs it,) before they came to dividing the conquered
lands, they did always very maturely
deliberate under what form or model of government they meant to live ; and accordingly made the partition of the poſſeſſions.
Moſes, Theſeus, and Romulus, founders of
Democracies, divided the land equally. Lycurgus, who meant an Optimacy, made a
certain number of ſhares which he intended to be in the hands of the people of Laconia. Cyrus, and other conquering monarchs before him, took all for themſelves and
ſucceſſors : which is obſerved in thoſe eaſ-
tern countries to this day ; and which has
made thoſe countries continue ever ſince
under the ſame government, though conquered and poſſeſſed very often by ſeveral
nations. This brings me to the ſecond
thing to be obſerved ; which is, " that
" wherever this apportionment of lands
" came to be changed in any kind, the go-
" vernment either changed with it, or was
" wholly in a ſtate of confuſion. " And for
this reaſon Lycurgus, the greateſt politician
that ever founded any government, took a
ſure way to fix property, by confounding it

D 3 and

and bringing all into common : and so the whole number of the natural Spartans, who inhabited the city of Lacedemon, eat and drank in their several convives together: and as long as they continued so to do, they did not only preserve their government entire (and that for a longer time than we can read of any commonwealth, that ever lasted a-mongst the ancients,) but held as it were the principality of Greece. The Athenians, for want of some constitutions to fix pro-perty as Theseus placed it, were in danger of utter ruin ; which they had certainly en-counter'd, if the good genius (as they then call'd it) of that people, had not raised them up a second founder, (more than six hun-dred years after the first,) which was Solon. And because the history of this matter will very much conduce to the illustrating of this aphorism we have laid down, I will presume so much upon your patience as to make a short recital of it ; leaving you to see it more at large, in Plutarch, and other au-thors. The lands in the territory of Attica, which were in the possession of the common people, (for what reason history is silent) were for debt all mortgaged to the great men

of

of the city of Athens; and the owners having no poffibility of redeeming their eftates,
were treating to compound with their creditors and deliver up their lands to them.
Solon (who was one of thofe ftate phyficians
we fpake of,) was much troubled at this,
and harangued daily to the nobility and people againft it; telling them firft, that it was
impoffible for the Grecians to refift the
Medes (who were then growing up to a
powerful monarchy) except Athens, the fecond city of Greece, did countenance a Democracy: that it was as impoffible the people could keep their empire, except they
kept their lands; nothing being more contrary to nature, than that thofe who poffefs
nothing in a country fhould pretend to govern it. They were all fenfible of his reafons, and of their own danger; but the only
remedy (which was, that the great men
fhould forgive the common people their
debts) would not at all be digefted. So that
the whole city (now fully underftanding their
condition) were continually in an uproar;
and the people flock'd about Solon, whenever he came abroad, defiring him to take
upon him the government and be their

prince;

prince; and they would make choice of him the next time they affembled. He told them, No, he would never be a tyrant, efpecially in his own country : meaning, that he who had no more fhare than other of the nobles, could not govern the reft, without being an ufurper or tyrant. But this he did to oblige his citizens; he frankly forgave all the debts that any of the people owed to him, and re-leafed their lands immediately : and this a-mounted to fifteen Attick talents of gold, (a vaft fum in thofe days;) and betook him-felf to a voluntary exile; in which he vifited Thales, and went to the oracle of Delphos, and offered up his prayers to Apollo for the prefervation of his city. In return of which (as the people then believed) the hearts of the great ones were fo changed and inlarged, that they readily agreed to remit all their debts to the people; upon condition, that Solon would take the pains to make them a new model of government, and laws fuita-ble to a Democracy; which he as readily ac-cepted and performed. By virtue of which that city grew and continued long the great-eft, the jufteft, the moft virtuous, learned and renowned, of all in that age : drove the

Perfians

Perſians afterwards out of Greece; defeated them both by ſea and land, with a quarter of their number of ſhips and men; and produced the greateſt wits and philoſophers that ever lived upon earth. The city of Athens inſtituted a ſolemn feaſt in commemoration of that great generoſity and ſelf-denial of the nobility; who ſacrificed their own intereſt to the preſervation of their country : which feaſt was called the ſolemnity of the Seiſactheia, (which ſignifies reciſion or abolition of debts,) and was obſerved with proceſſions, ſacrifices, and games, till the time of the Romans dominion over them (who encouraged it) and even till the change of religion in Greece, and invaſion of the Sarazens. The Romans, having omitted in their inſtitution to provide for the fixing of property, and ſo the nobility (called Patricii) beginning to take to themſelves a greater ſhare in the conquer'd lands than had been uſual (for in the firſt times of the commonwealth under Romulus, and ever after, it was always practiſed to divide the lands equally amongſt the tribes) this innovation ſtirred up Licinius Stolo, then tribune of the people, to propoſe a law (which, although it met with

D 5

much

much difficulty, yet at laſt was conſented to) by which it was provided, that no Roman citizen, of what degree ſoever, ſhould poſſeſs above five hundred acres of land; and for the remaining part of the lands which ſhould be conquer'd, it was ordered to be equally divided, as formerly, amongſt the tribes. This found admittance (after much oppoſition) becauſe it did provide but for the future; no man at that time being owner of more lands, than what was lawful for him to poſſeſs: and if this law had been ſtrictly obſerved to the laſt, that glorious commonwealth might have ſubſiſted to this day, for aught we know.

Doct. Some other cauſe would have been the ruin of it: what think you of a foreign conqueſt?

Eng. Gent. Oh doctor, if they had kept their poverty, they had kept their government and their virtue too; and then it had not been an eaſy matter to ſubdue them: *Quos vult perdere Jupiter, dementat.* Breach of rules and order cauſes diviſion; and diviſion, when it comes to be incurable, expoſes a nation, almoſt as much as a tyrannical-government does. The Goths and Vandals,

Vandals, had they invaded in those days, had met with the same fuccefs which befel the Cymbri and the Teutones. I muft confefs, a foreign invafion is a formidable thing, when a commonwealth is weak in territory and inhabitants, and that the invader is numerous and warlike ; and fo we fee the Romans were in danger of utter ruin, when they were firft attacked by the Gauls under Brennus. The like hazard may be fear'd, when a commonwealth is affaulted by another of equal virtue, and a commander of equal addrefs and valour to any of themfelves ; thus the Romans ran the rifk of their liberty and empire, in the war of Hannibal : but their power and their virtue grew to that heighth in that conteft, that when it was ended, I believe, that if they had preferved the foundation of their government entire, they had been invincible. And if I were alone of this opinion, I might be afhamed ; but I am back'd by the judgment of your incomparable country-man Machiavil : and no man will condemn either of us of rafhnefs, if he firft confiders what fmall ftates, that have ftood upon right bottoms, have done to defend their liberty againft

great

great monarchs. As is to be feen in the
example of the little commonwealth of
Athens; which deftroyed the fleet of Xerxes, confifting of a thoufand veffels, in the
ftreights of Salamis : and before, the land-
army of Darius, of three hundred thoufand,
in the plains of Marathon, and drove them
out of Greece : for though the whole confederates were prefent at the battle of Pla-
tæa, yet the Athenian army fingly under
their general Miltiades gain'd that renowned
battle of Marathon.

Noble Ven. I befeech you, fir, how was
it poffible, or practicable, that the Romans
conquering fo many and fo remote provinces, fhould yet have been able to preferve their Agrarian law, and divide all thofe
lands equally to their citizens ? or if it had
been poffible, yet it would have ruin'd their
city, by fending all their inhabitants away;
and by taking in ftrangers in their room,
they muft neceffarily have had people lefs
virtuous and lefs warlike ; and fo both their
government and their military difcipline
muft have been corrupted : for it is not to
be imagined, but that the people would
have gone with their families to the place
where

where their lands lay : so that it appears that the Romans did not provide, in the making and framing their first polity, for so great conquests as they afterwards made.

Eng. Gen. Yes, surely they did : from their first beginning, they were founded in war, and had neither land nor wives but what they fought for ; but yet what you object were very weighty, if there had not been a consideration of that early : for as soon as that great and wife people had subdued the Samnites on the east, and brought their arms as far as the Greek plantations, in that part of Italy which is now called the kingdom of Naples ; and westward, had reduced all the Tuscans under their obedience, as far as the river Arnus ; they made that, and the river Volturnus, (which runs by the walls of Capua,) the two boundaries of their empire, which was called *Domicilium Imperii.* These were the *ne plus ultra* ; for what they conquered between these two rivers, was all confiscated and divided amongst the tribes ; the Rustick tribes being twenty-seven, and the Urbane tribes nine, which made thirty-six in all. The City tribes were like our companies in London, consisting

fifting of tradefmen. The Country tribes
were divided like fhires; and there was
fcarce any landed man who inhabited in the
city, but he was written in that tribe where
his eftate lay : fo that the Ruftick tribes
(though they had all equal voices) were of
far more credit and reputation than the Urbane. Upon the days of the Comitia, which
were very well known, as many as thought
fit amongft the country tribes came to give
their voices; though every tribe was very
numerous of inhabitants, that lived in the
city. Now the Agrarian did not extend to
any lands conquered beyond this precinct,
but they were left to the inhabitants; they
paying a revenue to the commonwealth :
all but thofe which were thought fit to be
fet out to maintain a Roman colony ; which
was a good number of Roman citizens, fent
thither, and provided of lands and habitations : which being armed, did ferve in the
nature of à citadel and garrifon to keep the
province in obedience ; and a Roman prae-
tor, proconful, or other governor, was fent
yearly to head them, and brought forces
with him befides. Now it was ever lawful
for any Roman citizen to purchafe what
                                          lands

lands he pleafed in any of thefe provinces ;
it not being dangerous to a city to have
their people rich, but to have fuch a power
in the governing part of the empire, as
fhould make thofe who managed the affairs
of the commonwealth depend upon them ;
which came afterwards to be that which
ruined their liberty, and which the Gracchi
endeavoured to prevent when it was too
late. For thofe illuftrious perfons, feeing
the diforder that was then in the commonwealth, and rightly comprehending the reafon, which was the intermiffion of the Agrarian, and by confequence the great purchafes
which were made by the men of Rome
(who had inriched themfelves in Afia and
the other provinces) in that part of Italy
which was between the two rivers before-
mentioned, began to harangue the people,
in hopes to perfuade them to admit of the
right remedy ; which was to confirm the
Agrarian law with a retrofpect ; which although they carried, yet the difficulties in
the execution proved fo great, that it never
took effect : by reafon that the common
people whofe intereft it was to have their
lands reftored, yet having long lived as clients

ents and dependents of the great ones, chose rather to depend still upon their patrons than to hazard all for an imaginary deliverance: by which supineness in them, they were prevail'd with rather to join (for the most part) with the oppressors of themselves and their country, and to cut the throats of their redeemers, than to employ their just resentment against the covetous violators of their government and property. So perished the two renowned Gracchi, one soon after the other; not for any crime, but for having endeavoured to preserve and restore their commonwealth: for which (if they had lived in times suitable to such an heroick undertaking, and that the virtue of their ancestors had been yet in any kind remaining) they would have merited and enjoyed a reputation equal to that of Lycurgus, or Solon; whereas as it happen'd they were sometime after branded with the name of sedition, by certain wits, who prostituted the noble flame of poetry (which before had wont to be employed in magnifying heroick actions) to flatter the lust and ambition of the Roman tyrants.

Noble

Noble Ven. Sir, I approve what you fay in all things; and in confirmation of it, fhall further alledge the two famous princes of Sparta, Agis and Cleomines: which I couple together, fince Plutarch does fo. Thefe (finding the corruption of their commonwealth, and the decay of their ancient virtue, to proceed from the neglect and inobfervance of their founders rules, and a breach of that equality which was firft inftituted ;) endeavoured to reftore the laws of Lycurgus, and divide the territory anew; their victory in the Peloponnefian war, and the riches and luxury brought into their city by Lyfander, having long before broken all the orders of their commonwealth, and deftroyed the proportions of land alloted to each of the natural Spartans. But the firft of thefe two excellent patriots perifhed by treachery, in the beginning of his enterprize: the other began and went on with incomparable prudence and refolution ;. but mifcarried afterwards, by the iniquity of the times, and bafenefs and wickednefs of the people. So infallibly true it is, that where the policy is corrupted, there muft neceffarily be alfo a corruption and depravation

vation of manners ; and an utter abolition
of all faith, juſtice, honour, and morality.
But I forget myſelf, and intrench upon your
province : there is nothing now remains to
keep you from the modern policies, but
that you pleaſe to ſhut up this diſcourſe of
the ancient governments, with ſaying ſome-
thing of the corruptions of Ariſtocracy and
Democracy. For I believe both of us are
ſatisfied that you have abundantly proved
your aſſertion : and that when we have lei-
ſure to examine all the ſtates or policies that
ever were, we ſhall find all their changes
to have turn'd upon this hinge of property ;
and that the fixing of that with good laws
in the beginning or firſt inſtitution of a
ſtate, and the holding to thoſe laws afterwards, is the only way to make a commonwealth immortal.

Eng. Gent. I think you are very right:
but I ſhall obey you ; and do preſume to differ from Ariſtotle, in thinking that he has
not fitly called thoſe extreams (for ſo I
will ſtile them) of Ariſtocracy and Democracy, corruptions : for that they do not
proceed from the alteration of property,
which is the *unica corruptio politica.* For
example,

example, I do not find that Oligarchy, or government of a few, which is the extream of an Optimacy, ever did arife from a few mens getting into their hands the eftates of all the reft of the nobility : for had it began fo, it might have lafted, which I never read of any that did. I will therefore conclude, that they were all tyrannies ; for fo the Greeks called all ufurpations, whether of one or more perfons : and all thofe that I ever read of, as they came in either by craft or violence, (as the thirty tyrants of Athens ; the fifteen of Thebes ; and the *Decem-viri* of Rome, though thefe at firft came in lawfully :) fo they were foon driven out ; and ever, were either aſſaſſinated, or died by the fword of juftice : and therefore I fhall fay no more of them ; not thinking them worth the name of a government. As for the extream of Democracy, which is Anarchy, it is not fo : for many commonwealths have lafted for a good time under that adminiftration (if I may fo call a ftate fo full of confufion.) An Anarchy then is, when the people not contented with their fhare in the adminiftration of the government, (which is the right of approving, or dif-

difapproving of laws, of leagues, and of making of war and peace, of judging in all caufes upon an appeal to them, and chufing all manner of officers) will take upon themfelves the office of the fenate too, in managing fubordinate matters of ftate, propofing laws originally, and affuming debate in the market-place, making their orators their leaders : nay, not content with this, will take upon them to alter all the orders of the government when they pleafe ; as was frequently practifed in Athens, and in the modern ftate of Florence. In both thefe cities, whenever any great perfon who could lead the people, had a mind to alter the government, he call'd them together, and made them vote a change. In Florence they call'd it ; *Chiamar il popolo a parlamento, e ripigliar lo ftato* ; which is fummoning the people into the market-place to refume the government ; and did then prefently inftitute a new one, with new orders, new magiftracies, and the like. Now that which originally caufes this diforder, is the admitting (in the beginning of a government, or afterwards) the meaner fort of people, who have no fhare in the territory, into an equal

part

part of ordering the commonwealth : thefe being lefs fober, lefs confidering, and lefs careful of the publick concerns ; and being commonly the major part ; are made the inftruments oft-times of the ambition of the great ones, and very apt to kindle into faction. But notwithftanding all the confufion which we fee under an Anarchy, (where the wifdom of the better fort is made ufelefs by the fury of the people ;) yet many cities have fubfifted hundreds of years in this condition : and have been more confiderable, and performed greater actions, than ever any government of equal extent did ; except it were a well-regulated Democracy. But it is true, they ruin in the end ; and that never by cowardice or bafenefs, but by too much boldnefs and temerarious undertakings ; as both Athens and Florence did : the firft undertaking the invafion of Sicily, when their affairs went ill elfewhere ; and the other, by provoking the Spaniard and the Pope. But I have done now ; and fhall pafs to fay fomething of the modern policies.

Noble Ven. Before you come to that, fir, pray fatisfy me in a point, which I fhould
have

have moved before but that I was unwilling to interrupt your rational difcourfe. How came you to take it for granted, that Mofes, Thefeus, and Romulus were founders of popular governments ? As for Mofes, we have his ftory written by an infallible pen. Thefeus was ever called king of Athens, though he liv'd fo long fince that what is written of him is juftly efteem'd fabulous : but Romulus certainly was a king ; and that government continued a monarchy, though elective, under feven princes.

Eng. Gent. I will be very fhort in my anfwer ; and fay nothing of Thefeus, for the reafon you are pleafed to alledge : but for Mofes, you may read in holy writ, that when, by God's command he had brought the Ifraelites out of Egypt, he did at firft manage them by acquainting the people with the eftate of their government ; which people were called together with the found of a trumpet, and are termed in fcripture the Congregation of the Lord. This government he thought might ferve their turn in their paffage ; and that it would be time enough to make them a better, when they were in poffeffion of the land of Canaan : efpecially

having

having made them judges and magiftrates at the inftance of his father-in-law; which are called in authors, *Præfecti Jethroniani*. But finding that this provifion was not fufficient, he complained to God, of the difficulty he had to make that ftate of affairs hold together. God was pleafed to order him, to let feventy elders be appointed for a fenate; but yet the Congregation of the Lord continued ftill and acted: and by the feveral foundings of the trumpets, either the fenate, or popular affembly were called together, or both. So that this government was the fame with all other Democracies; confifting of a principal magiftrate, a fenate, and a people affembled together: not by reprefentation, but in a body. Now for Romulus; it is very plain, that he was no more than the firft officer of the commonwealth (whatever he was called,) and that he was chofen (as your Doge is,) for life. And when the laft of thofe feven kings ufurp'd the place; that is, did reign *injuffu populi* and exercife the government tyrannically; the people drove him out, (as all people in the world that have property will do in the like cafe, except fome extraordinary qualifi-

2 cations

cations in the prince preserve him for one age) and afterwards appointed in his room two magiftrates, and made them annual; which two had the fame command as well in their armies, as in their cities; and did not make the leaft alteration befides; excepting that they chofe an officer that was to perform the king's function, in certain facrifices which Numa appointed to be performed by the king; left the people fhould think their religion was changed: this officer was called *rex facrificulus*. If you are fatisfied; I will go on to the confideration of our modern ftates.

Noble Ven. I am fully anfwered; and befides am clearly of opinion, that no government, whether mixt monarchy or commonwealth, can fubfift without a fenate: as well from the turbulent ftate of the Ifraelites under Mofes, till the Sanhedrim was inftituted; as from a certain kingdom of the Vandals in Africa; where, after their conqueft of the natives, they appointed a government confifting of a prince and a popular affembly; which latter, within half a year, beat the king's brains out; he having no bulwark

wark of nobility, or senate, to defend him from them. But I will divert you no longer.

Eng. Gent. Sir, you are very right; and we should have spoken something of that before, if it had been the business of this meeting to discourse of the particular models of government : but intending only to say so much of the ancient policy as to shew what Government in general · is, and upon what basis it stands ; I think I have done it sufficiently to make way for the understanding of our own ; at least, when I have said something of the policies which are now extant; and that, with your favour, I will do. I shall need say little now of those commonwealths, which however they came by their liberty, either by arms or purchase, are now much-what under the same kind of policy as the ancients were. In Germany, the free towns, and many princes, make up the body of a commonwealth, called the empire ; of which the emperour is head. This general union hath its diets or parliaments, where they are all represented ; and where all things concerning the safety and interest of Germany in general, or that belong to

E   peace

peace and war, are transacted. These diets never intermeddle with the particular concerns or policies of those princes or states that make it up, leaving to them their particular soveraignties. The several imperial cities, or commonwealths, are divided into two kinds; Lubeck's law, and Collen's law: which being the same exactly with the ancient Democracies and Optimacies, I will say no more of them. The governments of Swizerland, and the seven provinces of the Low-countries, were made up in haste; to unite them against persecution and oppression, and to help to defend themselves the better: which they both have done very gallantly and succesfully. They seem to have taken their pattern from the Grecians; who, when their greatness began to decline, and the several tyrants who succeeded Alexander began to press hard upon them, were forced to league themselves (yet in several confederacies, as that of the Etolians, that of the Achaians, &c.) for their mutual defence. The Swisses consist of thirteen soveraignties; some cities, which are most Aristocratical; and some provinces, which have but a village for their head township.

These

These are all Democracies ; and are govern'd all, by the owners of land : who assemble, as our freeholders do, at the county-court. They have their general diets, as in Germany. The government of the united provinces has for its foundation the union of Utrecht ; made in the beginning of their standing upon their guard against the cruelty and oppression of the Spaniard, and patcht up in haste ; and seeming to be compos'd only for necessity as a state of war, has made modern statesmen conjecture, that it will not be very practicable in time of peace and security. At their general diet (which is called the States General) do intervene the deputies of the seven provinces, in what number their principals please : but all of them have but one vote, which are by consequence seven ; and every one of the seven hath a negative : so that nothing can pass without the concurrence of the whole seven. Every one of these provinces have a council or assembly of their own, called the States Provincial, who send and instruct their deputies to the states general ; and perform other offices belonging to the peace and quiet of the province. These deputies to the

states

states provincial, are sent by the several cities of which every province consists, and
by the nobility of the province, which hath
one voice only.   The basis of the government lies in these cities ; which are each of
them a distinct soveraignty : neither can the
states of the province, much less the states
general, intrench in the least upon their
rights, nor so much as intermeddle with
the government of their cities, or administration of justice; but only treat of
what concerns their mutual defence, and
their payments towards it.   Every one of
these cities is a soveraignty ; governed by an
Optimacy, consisting of the chief citizens : which upon death are supplyed by
new ones elected by themselves.   These are
called the Urnuscaperie, or Herne ; which
council has continued to govern those towns,
time out of mind : even in the times of
their Princes, who were then the soveraigns:
for without the consent of him, or his deputy, called state-holder, nothing could be
concluded in those days.   Since, they have
instituted an artificial minister of their own,
whom they still call state-holder ; and make
choice of him in their provincial assemblies,
                                          and

and for form fake defer fomething to him,
as the approbation of their *Skepen* and other
magiftrates, and fome other matters. This
has been continued in the province of Holland, which is the chief province, in the
fucceffion of the princes of Orange ; and in
the moft of the others too : the reft have
likewife chofen fome other of the houfe of
Naffaw. This government (fo oddly fet together, and fo compos'd of a ftate intended
for a monarchy ; and which as almanacks
calculated for one meridian are made in
fome fort to ferve for another, is by them
continued in thefe feveral Ariftocracies) may
laft for a time : till peace and fecurity, together with the abufe which is like to happen in the choice of the Herne, when they
fhall elect perfons of fmall note into their
body upon vacancies, for kindred or relation, rather than fuch as are of eftate and
eminency, or that otherwife abufe their power in the execution of it ; and then it is believed, and reafonably enough, that thofe
people (great in wealth, and very acute in
the knowledge of their own intereft) will
find out a better form of government ; or
make themfelves a prey to fome great neigh-

bour-prince

bour-prince in the attempting it: and this in case they in the mean time escape conquest from this great and powerful king of France, who at this time gives law to Christendom. I have nothing now left to keep me from the modern monarchies, but the most famous commonwealth of Venice; of which it would be presumption for me to say any thing, whilst you are present.

Noble Ven. You may very safely go on if you please: for I believe strangers understand the speculative part of our government better than we do; and the doctrine of the ballot, which is our chief excellency: for I have read many descriptions of our frame, which have taught me something in it which I knew not before; particularly, Donato Gianotti the Florentine, to whom I refer those who are curious to know more of our orders. For we that manage the mechanical part of the government, are like horses who know their track well enough, without considering East or West, or what business they go about. Besides, it would be very tedious, and very needless, to make any relation of our model, with the several councils that make it up; and would be

that

that which you have not done in treating of
any other government. What we have faid
is enough to fhew what beginning we had ;
and that ferves your turn : for we who are
called nobility, and who manage the ftate,
are the defcendents of the firft inhabitants ;
and had therefore been a democracy, if a
numerous flock of ftrangers (who are contented to come and live among us as fubjects) had
not fwelled our city, and made the governing party feem but a handfull. So that we
have the fame foundations that all other Ari_
ftocracies have, who govern but one city; and
have no territory, but what they govern pro-
vincially. And our people, not knowing
where to have better juftice, are very well
contented to live amongft us ; without any
fhare in the managing of affairs. Yet we have
power to adopt whom we pleafe into our
nobility : and I believe that in the time of
the Roman greatnefs, there were five for
one of the inhabitants who were written
in no tribe, but look'd upon as ftrangers,
and yet that did not vitiate their democracy ; no more than our citizens and common people can hurt our optimacy. All
the difficulty in our adminiftration, hath

been

been to regulate our own nobility, and to bridle their faction and ambition ; which can alone breed a difeafe in the vital part of our government : and this we do, by moft fevere laws ; and a very rigorus execution of them.

Doct. Sir, I was thinking to interpofe concerning the propriety of lands in the territory of Padua ; which, I hear, is wholly in the poffeffion of the nobility of Venice.

Noble Ven. Our members have very good eftates there, yet nothing but what they have paid very well for ; no part of that country, or of any other province, having been fhar'd amongft us as in other conquefts. 'Tis true, that the Paduans having ever been the moft revengeful people of Italy, could not be deterr'd from thofe execrable and treacherous murders, which were every day commited, but by a fevere execution of the laws as well againft their lives as eftates : and as many of their eftates as were confifcated, were (during our neceffities in the laft war with the Turks) expofed to fale, and fold to them that offered moft ; without any confideration of the perfons purchafing. But it is very true, that moft of them came into the hands of our
nobility ;

nobility; they offering more than any o-
ther: by reason that their sober and frugal
living, and their being forbidden all manner
of traffick, makes them have no way of
employing the money which proceeds from
their parsimony; and so they can afford
to give more than others, who may employ
their advance to better profit elsewhere. But
I perceive, doctor, by this question, that
you have studied at Padua.

Doct. No really, sir, the small learning
I have was acquired in our university of Oxford; nor was I ever out of this island.

Noble Ven. I would you had, sir; for it
would have been a great honour to our
country to have contributed any thing towards so vast a knowledge as you are pos-
sessor of: but I wish that it were your country, or at least the place of your habitation,
that so we might partake not only of your excellent discourse sometimes, but be the better
for your skill; which would make us immortal.

Doct. I am glad to see you so well that
you can make your self so merry: but I af-
sure you I am very well here. England is
a good wholsome climate for a physician.
But, pray let our friend go on to his modern
monarchies.

Eng.

Eng. Gent. This is all I have now to do. Thofe monarchies are two, abfolute, and mixt. For the firft kind, all that we have knowledge of except the empire of the Turks, differ fo little from the ancient monarchies of the Aſſyrians and Perſians ; that having given a ſhort defcription of them before, it will be needlefs to fay any more of the Perfian, the Mogul, the King of Pegu, China, Preſtor-John ; or any other the great men under thofe princes, as the Satrapes of old : being made fo, only by their being employed and put into great places and governments by the foveraign. But the monarchy of the grand feignior is fomething different. They both ageee in this, that the prince is in both abfolute proprietor of all the lands, (excepting in the kingdom of Egypt, of which I ſhall fay fomething anon ;) but the diverfity lies in the adminiftration of the property : the other emperofs as well ancient as modern uſing to manage the revenue of the feveral towns and parifhes, as our kings or the kings of France do ; that is, keep it in their hands, and adminifter it by officers : and fo you may read that Xerxes king of Perfia allowed the revenue of fo many

I

villages

villages to Themiſtocles; which affignations are practiſed at this day, both to publick and to private uſes, by the preſent monarchs. But the Turks, when they invaded the broken empire of the Arabians, did not at firſt make any great alteration in their policy : till the houſe of Ottoman, the preſent royal family, did make great conqueſts in Aſia, and afterwards in Greece : whence they might poſſibly take their preſent way of dividing their conquered territories ; for they took the ſame courſe which the Goths and other modern people had uſed with their conquered lands in Europe, upon which they planted military colonies, by dividing them amongſt the ſoldiers for their pay or maintenance. Theſe ſhares were called by them Timarrs, which ſignifies benefices : and differ'd in this only from the European knights-fees, that theſe laſt originally were hereditary, and ſo property was maintained; whereas amongſt the Ottomans, they were meerly at will ; and they enjoyed their ſhares whilſt they remained the Sultan's ſoldiers, and no longer ; being turn'd out both of his ſervice, and of their Timarrs, when he pleaſes. This doubtleſs had been the beſt

E 6　　　　　　　　and

and firmeſt monarchy in the world, if they
could have ſtayed here, and not had a merce-
nary army beſides; which have often (like the
prætorians in the time of the Roman tyrants)
made the palace and the ſeraglio the ſham-
bles of their princes; whereas if the Timar-
riots, as well Spahis (or horſe) as foot, had
been brought together to guard the prince
by courſes (as they uſed to do king David)
as well as they are to fight for the empire;
this horrid flaw and inconvenience in their
government had been wholly avoided. For
though theſe are not planted upon entire
property, as David's were; (thoſe being in
the nature of trained-bands;) yet the re-
moteneſs of their habitations from the court
and the factions of the great city, and their
deſire to repair home and to find all things
quiet at their return, would have eaſily kept
them from being infected with that curſed
diſeaſe of rebellion againſt their ſoveraign,
upon whoſe favour they depend for the continuance of their livelihood: whereas the
Janizaries are for life, and are ſure to be in
the ſame employment under the next ſuc-
ceſſor: ſo ſure, that no grand ſeignior can,
or dares go about to diſband them; the ſuſ-
picion

picion of intending fuch a thing having caufed the death of more than one of their emperors.   But I fhall go to the limited Monarchies.

Doct. But pray, before you do fo, inform us fomething of the Roman emperors : had they the whole dominion or property of the lands of Italy ?

Eng. Gent. The Roman emperors I reckon amongft the tyrants : for fo amongft the Greeks were called thofe citizens who ufurp'd the government of their commonwealths, and maintain'd it by force, without endeavouring to found or eftablifh it, by altering the property of lands, as not imagining that their children could ever hold it after them ; in which they were not deceived : fo that it was plain that the Roman empire was not a natural but a violent government. The reafons why it lafted longer than ordinarily tyrannies do, are many.   Firft, becaufe Auguftus the firft emperor kept up the fenate, and fo for his time cajol'd them with this bait of imaginary power ; which might not have fufficed neither to have kept him from the fate of his uncle, but that there had been fo many revolutions and bloody

wars

wars between, that all mankind was glad to repose and take breath for a while under any government that could protect them. And he gain'd the service of these senators the rather, because he suffered none to be so but those who had followed his fortune in the several civil wars; and so were engaged to support him for their own preservation: besides, he confiscated all those who had at any time been proscribed, or sided in any encounter against him; which, considering in how few hands the lands of Italy then were, might be an over-balance of the property in his hands. But this is certain; that whatever he had not in his own possession, he disposed of at his pleasure; taking it away, as also the lives of his people, without any judicial proceedings, when he pleased. That the confiscations were great, we may see by his planting above sixty thousand soldiers upon lands in Lombardy; that is, erecting so many beneficia, or timarrs: and, if any man's lands lay in the way, he took them in for neighbourhood, without any delinquency. *Mantua væ miseræ nimium vicina Cremonæ.* And it is very evident, that if these beneficia had not after-

wards

wards been made hereditary, that empire might have had a ftabler foundation ; and fo a more quiet and orderly progrefs than it after had : for the court-guards, call'd the prætorians, did make fuch havock of their princes, and change them fo often, that this (though it may feem a paradox) is another reafon why this tyranny was not ruin'd fooner. For the people, who had really an intereft to endeavour a change of government, were fo prevented by feeing the prince whom they defigned to fupplant, removed to their hand, that they were puzzled what to do ; taking in the mean time great recreation to fee thofe wild beafts hunted down themfelves, who had fo often prey'd upon their lives and eftates : befides that, moft commonly the frequent removes of their mafters, made them fcarce have time to do any mifchief to their oppreffed fubjects in particular, though they were all flaves in general. This government of the later Romans is a clear example of the truth and efficacy of thefe politick principles we have been difcourfing of. Firft, that any government (be it the moft unlimited and arbitrary Monarchy) that is placed upon a

right

right basis of property, is better both for prince and people, than to leave them a seeming property still at his devotion ; and then for want of fixing the foundation, expose their lives to those dangers and hazzards, with which so many tumults and infurrections, which must necessarily happen, will threaten them daily. And in the next place, that any violent constraining of mankind to a subjection, is not to be called a government ; nor does salve either the politick or moral ends, which those eminent legislators amongst the ancients proposed to themselves, when they set rules to preserve the quiet and peace, as well as the plenty prosperity and greatness of the people ; but that the politicks, or art of governing, is a science to be learned and studied by counsellors and statesmen be they never so great : or else mankind will have a very sad condition under them, and they themselves a very perplexed and turbulent life, and probably a very destructive and precipitous end of it.

Doct. I am very glad I gave occasion to make this discourse : now I beseech you,

before

before you go to the mix'd Monarchies, not to forget Egypt.

Eng. Gent. 'Twas that I was coming to, before you were pleafed to interrogate me concerning the Roman empire. The Egyptians are this day, for aught I know, the only people that enjoy property, and are governed as a province, by any of the eaftern abfolute princes. For whereas Damafco, Aleppo, and moft of the other cities and provinces of that empire, whofe territory is divided into timarrs, are governed by a bafhaw, who for his guards has fome fmall number of janizaries or foldiers; the bafhaw of Egypt, or of Grand Cairo, has ever an army with him: and divers forts are erected; which is the way European princes ufe in governing their provinces; and muft be fo where property is left entire, except they plant colonies as the Romans did. The reafon why Selim, who broke the empire of the Mamalukes, and conquered Egypt, did not plant timarrs upon it, was the lazinefs and cowardlinefs of the people, and the great fruitfulnefs of the foil, and delicioufnefs of the country, which has mollify'd and render'd

effe-

effeminate all the nations that ever did inhabit it. So that a resolution was taken to
impose upon them, first, the maintaining
an army by a tax; and then to pay a full
half of all the fruits and product of their
lands to the grand seignior, which they are
to cultivate and improve. This is well
managed by the bashaws and their officers;
and comes to an incredible sum: the goods
being sold, the money is conveyed in specie
to the port, and is the greatest part of that
prince's revenue. And it is believed, that
if all the lands had been entirely confiscated,
and that the grand seignior had managed
them by his officers, he would not have
made a third part so much of the whole, as
he receives now annually for one half: not
only because those people are extreamly in-
dustrious, where their own profit is concerned; but for that it is clear, if they had
been totally divested of their estates, they
would have left their country; and made
that which is now the most populous kingdom of the world, a desart: as is all the rest
of the Turkish dominions, except some cities.
And if the people had removed as they did
elsewhere, there would not only have wanted

ed hands to have cultivated and improved the lands, but mouths to confume the product of it ; fo that the prince's revenue by the cheapnefs of victual, and the want of labourers, would have almoft fallen to nothing.

Noble Ven. Pray God this be not the reafon that this king of France leaves property to his fubjects ; for certainly he hath taken example by this province of Egypt : his fubjects having a tax (which for the continuance of it, I muft call a rent or tribute) impos'd upon them, to the value of one full half of their eftates ; which muft ever increafe, as the lands improve.

Eng. Gent. I believe, fir, there is another reafon ; for the property there, being in the nobility and gentry, which are the hands by which he manages his force both at home and abroad, it would not have been eafy or fafe for him to take away their eftates.——But I come to the limited Monarchies. They were firft introduced (as was faid before) by the Goths, and other nothern people. Whence thofe great fwarms came, as it was unknown to Procopius himfelf who liv'd in the time of their invafion, and who
was

was a diligent searcher into all the circum-
stances of their concernments, so it is very
needless for us to make any enquiry into it ;
thus much being clear, that they came man
woman and child, and conquer'd and pos-
sess'd all these parts of the world ; which
were then subject to the Roman empire,
and since Christianity came in have been so
to the Latin church ; till honest John Cal-
vin taught some of us the way how to deliver ourselves from the tyrannical yoke,
which neither we nor our forefathers were
able to bear. Whence those people had the
government they establish'd in these parts
after their conquest ; that is, whether they
brought it from their own country, or made
it themselves ; must needs be uncertain,
since their original is wholly so : but it seems
very probable that they had some excellent
persons among them, though the ignorance
and want of learning in that age hath not
suffered any thing to remain that may give
us any great light ; for it is plain, that the
government they settled, was both according to the exact rules of the politicks, and
very natural and suitable to that division
they made of their several territories. Whenever

ever then thefe invaders had quieted any
province, and that the people were driven
out or fubdued, they divided the lands : and
to the prince they gave ufually a tenth part,
or thereabouts ; to the great men, or *co-
mites regis*, as it was tranflated into Latin,
every one, as near as they could, an equal
fhare. Thefe were to enjoy an hereditary
right in their eftates ; as the king did in
his part, and in the crown. But neither
he, nor his peers or companions, were to
have the abfolute difpofal of the lands fo allotted them : but were to keep a certain
proportion to themfelves for their ufe ; and
the reft was ordered to be divided amongft
the freemen, who came with them to conquer. What they kept to themfelves was
called demefnes, in Englifh and French ;
and in Italian, *beni allodiali*. The other
part which they granted to the freemen,
was called a feud : and all thefe eftates were
held of thefe lords hereditarily, only the tenants were to pay a fmall rent annually ;
and at every death or change an acknowledgment in money, and in fome tenures
the beft beaft befides. But the chief condition of the feud or grant, was, that the
tenant

tenant fhould perform certain fervices to the
lord ; of which one (in all tenures of freemen) was to follow him armed to the wars,
for the fervice of the prince and defence of
the land.   And upon their admittance to
their feuds, they took an oath to be true
vaffals and tenants to their lords ; and to
pay their rents, and perform their fervices;
and upon failure to forfeit their eftates. And
thefe tenants were divided, according to
their habitations, into feveral manors ; in
every one of which there was a court kept,
twice every year ; where they all were to
appear, and to be admitted to their feveral
eftates, and to take the oath above mentioned.   All thefe peers did likewife hold all
their demefnes, as alfo all their manors, of
the prince : to whom they fwore allegiance
and fealty.   There were befides thefe freemen or francklins, other tenants to every
lord, who were called villains ; who were
to perform all fervile offices, and their
eftates were all at the lord's difpofal when
he pleafed : thefe confifted moftly of fuch
of the former inhabitants of thefe countries,
as were not either deftroyed or driven out ;
and poffibly of others who were fervants
                                        amongft

amongst them, before they came from their own countries. Perhaps thus much might have been unneceffary to be faid; confidering that thefe lords, tenants, and courts, are yet extant in all the kingdoms in Europe : but that to a gentleman of Venice, where there are none of thefe things, and where the Goths never were, fomething may be faid in excufe for me.

Noble Ven. 'Tis true, fir, we fled from the Goths betimes; but yet in thofe countries which we recovered fince in *terra firma*, we found the footfteps of thefe lords, and tenures, and their titles of counts : tho' being now provinces to us, they have no influence upon the government; as, I fuppofe, you are about to prove they have in thefe parts.

Eng. Gent. You are right, fir; for the governments of France, Spain, England, and all other countries where thefe people fettled, were fram'd accordingly. It is not my bufinefs to defcribe particularly the diftinct forms of the feveral governments in Europe, which do derive from thefe people (for they may differ in fome of their orders and laws, though the foundation be in them

all

all the same) this would be unneceffary, they
being all extant and fo well known : and
befides, little to my purpofe ; excepting to
fhew where they have declined from their
firft inftitution, and admitted of fome change.
France, and Poland, have not, nor as I can
learn, ever had any freemen below the nobility ; that is, had no yeomen ; but all are
either noble, or villains : therefore the lands
muft have been originally given, as they
now remain, into the hands of thefe nobles.
But I will come to the adminiftration of the
government in thefe countries ; and firft
fay wherein they all agree, or did at leaft in
their inftitution ; which is, that the foveraign power is in the ftates affembled together by the prince, in which he prefides ;
thefe make laws, levy money, redrefs grievances, punifh great officers, and the like.
Thefe ftates confift in fome places of the
prince and nobility only, as in Poland ; and
anciently in France, before certain towns,
for the encouraging of trade, procured privileges to fend deputies : which deputies
are now called the third eftate : and in
others, confift of the nobility and commonalty ; which latter had, and ftill have the
-fame

fame right to intervene and vote, as the great ones have both in England, Spain, and other kingdoms.

Doct. But you fay nothing of the clergy : I fee you are no great friend to them, to leave them out of your politicks.

Eng. Gent. The truth is, doctor, I could wifh there had never been any : the purity of Chriftian religion, as alfo the good and orderly government of the world, had been much better provided for without them ; as it was in the apoftolical time, when we hear nothing of clergy : but my omitting their reverend lordfhips was no neglect, for I meant to come to them in order ; for you know that the northern people did not bring Chriftianity into thefe parts, but found it here, and were in time converted to it ; fo that there could be no clergy at the firft. But if I had faid nothing at all of this race, yet I had committed no folecifm in the politicks : for the bifhops and great abbots intervened in the ftates here, upon the fame foundation that the other peers do ; viz. for their great poffeffions, and the dependence their tenants and vaffals have upon them : although they being a people of that great fanctity and

F   knowledge,

knowledge, fcorn to intermix fo much as titles with us profane lay-idiots ; and therefore will be called, lords fpiritual. But you will have a very venerable opinion of them, if you do but confider how they came by thefe great poffeffions, which made them claim a third part of the government. And truly not unjuftly, by my rule ; for I believe they had no lefs (at one time) than a third part of the lands, in moft of thefe countries.

Noble Ven. Pray, how did they acquire thefe lands ? was it not here by the charitable donation of pious Chriftians, as it was elfewhere ?

Eng. Gent. Yes, certainly, very pious men ! fome of them might be well-meaning people, but ftill fuch as were cheated by thefe holy men : who told them perpetually, both in publick and private ; " that they " reprefented God upon earth, being or- " dained by authority from him who was " his viceroy here ; and that what was given " to them, was given to God ; and he would " repay it largely, both in this world, " and the next. " This wheedle made our barbarous anceftors, newly inftructed in the
Chriftian

Chriftian faith, (if this religion may be called fo, and fucking in this foolifh doctrine
more than the doctrine of Chrift) fo zealous
to thefe vipers, that they would have pluckt
out their eyes to ferve them ; much more
beftow, as they did, the fruitfulleft and beft
fituate of their poffeffions upon them. Nay,
fome they perfwaded to take upon them their
callings ; vow chaftity, and give all they had
to them ; and become one of them ; amongft
whom, I believe, they found no more fanctity, than they left in the world. But this
is nothing to another trick they had : which
was to infinuate into the moft notorious and
execrable villains with which that age a-
bounded ; men, who being princes, (and
other great men, for fuch were the tools
they work'd with) had treacheroufly poifon'd,
or otherwife murdered their neareft relations,
fathers, brothers, wives, to reign or enjoy
their eftates : thefe they did perfwade into a
belief, " that if they had a defire to be
" fav'd notwithftanding their execrable vil-
" lainies, they need but part with fome of
" thofe great poffeffions (*which they had ac-
" quired by thofe acts :*) to their bifhopricks
" or monafteries, and they would pray for

" their

" their fouls ; and they were fo holy and
" acceptable to God, that he would deny
" them nothing : " which they immediately performed ; fo great was the ignorance
and blindnefs of that age ! And you fhall
hardly find in the ftory of thofe times, any
great monaftery, abbey, or other religious
houfe in any of thefe countries, (I fpeak
confidently as to what concerns our own
Saxons,) that had not its foundation from
fome fuch original.

Doɕt. A worthy beginning, of a worthy
race !

Noble Ven. Sir, you maintain a ftrange
pofition here, that it had been better there
had been no clergy. Would you have had
no gofpel preached, no facraments, no continuance of Chriftian religion in the world ?
Or do you think that thefe things could
have been without a fucceffion of the
true priefthood, or (as you call it, of true
miniftry) by means of ordination ? Do's
not your own church hold the fame ?

Eng. Gent. You will know more of my
church, when I have told you what I find
the word church to fignifie in fcripture ;
which is to me, the only rule of faith, wor-
ſhip,

ship, and manners : neither do I seek these
additional helps, of fathers, councils, or ecclesiastical history ; much less tradition : for
since it is said in the word of God it self,
" that Antichrist did begin to work even in
" those days ; " I can easily believe that
he had brought his work to some perfection,
before the word church was by him applied
to the clergy. I shall therefore tell you what
I conceive that church, clergy, and ordination, signified in the apostolical times. I
find then the word, church, in the new
testament taken but in two senses : the first,
for the universal invisible church, called
sometimes of the first-born ; that is, the
whole number of the true followers of
Christ in the world, where-ever resident, or
into what part soever dispersed. The o-
ther signification of church, is an assembly ;
which though it be sometimes used to express any meetings (even unlawful and tu-
multuous ones) as well in scripture, as profane authors ; yet it is more frequently understood of a gathering together to the du-
ties of prayer, preaching, and breaking of
bread : and the whole number so congregated is, both in the acts of the apostles and

in

in their holy epiftles, called the Church.
Nor is there the leaft colour for appropriat-
ing that word to the paftors and deacons ;
who, fince the corruptions of chriftian religion,
are called clergy. Which word in the old
teftament is ufed, fometimes for God's whole
people, and fometimes for the tribe of Levi,
out of which the priefts were chofen : for
the word fignifies a lot ; fo that tribe is called God's lot, becaufe they had no fhare allotted them when the land was divided, but
were to live upon tythe, and ferve in the
functions of their religion, and be Singers,
Porters, Butchers, Bakers, and Cooks, for
the facrifices &c. So that this tribe was
ftiled clergy but figuratively ; and the alle-
gory paffed into the new teftament : where
the faints are fometimes called clergy ; but
never the paftors or deacons : who were far
from pretending, in thofe days, to come in
the place of the Aaronical priefthood.
The word Ordination, in fcripture, fignifies lifting up of hands ; and is ufed, firft,
for the giving a fuffrage, which in all popular affemblies was done by ftretching out
the hand (as it is in the common hall of
London :) in the next place, it is applied to
the

the order or decree made by the fuffrage
fo given ; which was then (and is yet too
in all modern languages) called an Ordi-
nance ; and the fuffrage it felf Ordination : which word proves that the firft
Chriftian churches were democratical ;
that is, that the whole congregation had
the choice in this, as well as the foveraign
authority in all excommunications, and all
other matters whatfoever that could occur :
for in all ariftocratical commonwealths the
word for choice is Keirothefia, or impofiti-
on of hands, (for fo the election of all magiftrates and officers was made,) and not
Keirotonia. Thefe paftors and other officers did not pretend to be, by virtue of fuch
choice, of a peculiar profeffion different
from other men ; as their followers have
done fince Antichrift's reign ; but were only
called and appointed (by the congregation's
approval of their gifts or parts) to inftruct
or feed the flock ; vifit the fick ; and perform all other offices of a true minifter
(that is, fervant) of the gofpel. At other
times, they followed the bufinefs of their
own trades and profeffions : and the Chriftians
in thofe times (which none will deny to have

been

been the pureft of the church) did never dream that a true paftor ought to pretend to any fucceffion, to qualifie him for the miniftry of the word ; or that the idle and ridiculous ceremonies ufed in your church, (and ftill continued in that which you are pleafed to call mine,) were any way effential or conducing to capacitate a perfon to be a true preacher or difpenfer of the Chriftian faith. And I cannot fufficiently admire why our clergy, who very juftly refufe to believe the miracle which is pretended to be wrought in Tranfubftantiation; becaufe they fee both the wafer and the wine to have the fame fubftance, and the fame accidents after the prieft has mumbled words over thofe elements as they had before; yet will believe, that the fame kind of fpell or charm in ordination can have the efficacy to metamorphofe a poor Lay-Idiot, into a heavenly creature : notwithftanding that we find in them the fame human nature, and the fame neceffities of it, to which they were fubject before fuch transformation; nay, the fame debauch, profanenefs, ignorance, and difability to preach the gofpel.

Noble

Noble Ven. Sir, this difcourfe is very new to me. I muft confefs I am much inclined to join with you in believing, that the power priefts exercife over mankind, with the jurifdiction they pretend to over princes and ftates, may be a ufurpation ; but that they fhould not have a divine call to ferve at the altar, or that any perfon can pretend to perform thofe facred functions without being duly ordained, feems very ftrange.

Eng. Gent. I am not now to difcourfe of Religion : it is never very civil to do fo in converfation of perfons of a different belief ; neither can it be of any benefit towards a Roman Catholick ; for if his confcience fhould be never fo clearly convinc'd, he is not yet mafter of his own faith ; having given it up to his church, of whom he muft afk leave to be a convert, which he will be fure never to obtain. But if you have the curiofity when you come amongft the learned in your own country (for amongft our ordination-mongers, there is a great fcarcity of letters and other good parts) you may pleafe to take the Bible, which you acknowledge to be the word of God as

F 5 well

well as we; and intreat fome of them to
fhew you any paffage, the plain and genuine fenfe of which can any way evince this
fucceffion, this ordination, or this priefthood, we are now fpeaking of: and when
you have done, if you will let your own
excellent reafon and difcourfe judge, and not
your prieft, (who is too much concerned in
point of intereft) I make no doubt but you
will be convinced that the pretence to the
difpenfing of divine things by virtue of a
human conftitution, and fo ridiculous a
one too as the ordination practifed by your
bifhops and ours, (who defcend and fucceed
from one and the fame mother) is as little
juftifiable by fcripture and reafon, and full
as great a cheat and ufurpation, as the empire which the ecclefiafticks pretend to over
the confciences and perfons of men, and the
exemption from all fecular power.

Noble Ven. Well, fir, though neither
my faith nor my reafon can come up to
what you hold, yet the novelty and the
grace of this argument has delighted me extreamly : and if that be a fin, as I fear it
is, I muft confefs it to my prieft ; but I afk
your

3

your pardon firſt, for putting you upon this long deviation.

Eng. Gent. Well, this digreſſion is not without its uſe : for it will ſhorten our buſineſs, (which is grown longer than I thought it would have been ;) for I ſhall mention the clergy no more : but whenever I ſpeak of peerage, pray take notice, that I mean both lords ſpiritual and temporal ; ſince they ſtand both upon the ſame foot of property. But if you pleaſe, I will fall immediately to diſcourſe of the government of England ; and ſay no more of thoſe of our neighbours, than what will fall in by the way, or be hinted to me by your demands : for the time runs away, and I know the doctor muſt be at home by noon, where he gives daily charitable audience to an infinity of poor people ; who have need of his help, and who ſend or come for it, not having the confidence to ſend for him, ſince they have nothing to give him : though he be very liberal too of his viſits to ſuch, where he has any knowledge of them. But I ſpare his modeſty, which I ſee is concerned at the juſt teſtimony I bear to his charity. The ſoveraign power of England then is in

king,

king, lords, and commons. The parliaments, as they are now conftituted (that
is, the afligning a choice to fuch a number
of burroughs, as alfo the manner and form
of elections and returns) did come in, as I
fuppofe, in the time of Henry the third;
where now our ftatute-book begins. And
I muft confefs. I was inclined to believe,
that before that time, our yeomanry or
commonalty had not formally affembled in
parliament, but been virtually included and
reprefented by the peers, upon whom they
depended : but I am fully convinced, that
it was otherwife, by the learned difcourfes
lately publifh'd by mr Petit of the Temple,
and mr Attwood of Grays-Inn ; being gentlemen whom I do mention, *honoris caufa.*
And really they deferve to be honour'd, that
they will fpare fome time from the mechanical part of their callings (which is to
affift clients with counfel, and to plead their
caufes, which I acknowledge likewife to be
honourable) to ftudy the true intereft of
their country ; and to fhew how ancient
the rights of the people in England are : and
that in a time, when neither profit nor
countenance can be hop'd for, from fo ingenious

genious an undertaking. But I beg pardon
for the deviation. Of the three branches
of foveraign power which politicians mention, which are enacting laws, levying of
taxes, and making war and peace, the two
firft of them are indifputably in the parliament; and when I fay parliament, I ever
intend, with the king. The laft, has been
ufually exercis'd by the prince; if he can
do it with his own money. Yet becaufe even
in that cafe it may be ruinous to the kingdom, by expofing it to an invafion, many
have affirmed that fuch a power cannot be
(by the true and ancient free government
of England) fuppofed to be intrufted in the
hands of one man; and therefore we fee in
divers kings reigns the parliament has been
confulted, and their advice taken in thofe
matters that have either concerned war or
leagues; and that if it has been omitted,
addreffes have been made to the king by
parliaments, either to make war, or peace;
according to what they thought profitable
to the publick. So that I will not determine whether that power which draws fuch
confequences after it, be by the genuine
fenfe of our laws in the prince or no; although

though I know of no ftatute, or written record, which makes it otherwife. That which is undoubtedly the king's right or prerogative, is to call and diffolve parliaments; to prefide in them; to approve of all acts made by them; and to put in execution, as fupream or foveraign magiftrate (in the intervals of parliaments, and during their fitting) all laws made by them, as alfo the common law. For which caufe he has the nomination of all inferior officers and minifters under him, excepting fuch as by law or charter are eligible otherwife; and the power of the fword, to force obedience to the judgments given both in criminal and civil caufes.

Doct. Sir, you have made us a very abfolute prince: what have we left us? If the king have all this power, what do our liberties or rights fignify, whenever he pleafes?

Eng. Gent. This objection, doctor, makes good what I faid before, that your fkill did not terminate in the body natural, but extended to the politick: for a more pertinent interrogatory could never have been made by Plato or Ariftotle. In anfwer to which, you

you may pleafe to underftand; that when
thefe conftitutions were firft made, our anceftors were a plain-hearted, well-meaning
people, without court-referves, or tricks;
who having made choice of this fort of government, and having power enough in
their hands to make it take place, did not
forefee or imagine, that any thoughts of
invading their rights could enter into the
prince's head. Nor do I read that it ever
did, till the Norman line came to reign:
which coming in by treaty, it was obvious
there was no conqueft made upon any but
Harold; in whofe ftead William the firft
came, and would claim no more after his
victory, than what Harold enjoy'd: excepting, that he might confifcate (as he did)
thofe great men who took part with the
wrong title; and Frenchmen were put into
their eftates. Which though it made in this
kingdom a mixture between Normans and
Saxons, yet produced no change or innovation in the government; the Norman peers
being as tenacious of their liberties, and as
active in the recovery of them to the full,
as the Saxon families were. Soon after the
death of William, (and poffibly, in his time,)
there

there began some invasions upon the rights of the kingdom; which begat grievances, and afterwards complaints and discontents: which grew to that height, that the peers were fain to use their power, that is, arm their vassals to defend the government; whilst the princes of that age, first king John, and then Henry the third, got force together. The barons call'd in Lewis the dauphin, (whilst the king would have given away the kingdom to the Sarazens, as he did to the Pope) and armed their own creatures; so that a bloody war ensued, for almost forty years off and on, as may be read in our history. The success was, that the barons or peers obtained, in the close, two charters or laws for the ascertaining their rights; by which, neither their lives, liberties, or estates, could ever be in danger any more from any arbitrary power in the prince: and so the good government of England, which was before this time (like the law of nature) only written in the hearts of men, came to be express'd in parchment and remain a record in writing; though these charters gave us no more, than what was our own before. After these char-

ters

ters were made, there could not chuse but
happen some encroachment upon them; but
so long as the peers kept their greatness,
there was no breaches but what were immediately made up in parliament: which whenever they assembled, did in the first place
confirm the charters, and made very often
interpretations upon them, for the benefit
of the people; witness the statute *de Talla-
gio non concedendo*, and many others. But
to come nearer the giving the doctor an answer, you may please to understand, that not
long after the framing of these foremen-
tioned charters, there did arise a grievance
not foreseen or provided for by them; and
it was such an one that had beaten down
the government at once, if it had not been
redressed in an orderly way. This was the
intermission of parliaments; which could
not be called but by the prince: and he not
doing of it, they ceast to be assembled for
some years. If this had not been speedily
remedied, the barons must have put on their
armour again: for who can imagine, that
such brisk assertors of their rights could have
acquiesced in an omission that ruined the
foundation of the government? which consisting

of king, lords, and commons, and having
at that time marched near five hundred years
upon three legs, muſt then have gone on
hopping upon one ; which could it have
gone forward (as was impoſſible, whilſt property continued where it was) yet would
have rid but a little way. Nor can it be
wonder'd at, that our great men made no
proviſion againſt this grievance in their charters : becauſe it was impoſſible for them to
imagine that their prince, who had ſo good
a ſhare in this government, ſhould go about
to deſtroy it, and to take that burden upon
himſelf ; which, by our conſtitution, was
undeniably to be divided between him and
his ſubjects. And therefore divers of the
great men of thoſe times ſpeaking with that
excellent prince king Edward the firſt about
it, he (to take away from his people all
fear and apprehenſion that he intended to
change the ancient government,) called
ſpeedily a parliament, and in it conſented
to a declaration of the kingdom's right in
that point : without the clearing of which,
all our other laws had been uſeleſs, and the
government itſelf too ; of which the parliament is (at the leaſt) as eſſential a part
as

as the prince. So that there paffed a law in that parliament, that one fhould be held every year; and oftner, if need be : which like another *Magna Charta*, was confirmed by a new act made in the time of Edward the third, that glorious prince. Nor were there any fycophants in thofe days, who durft pretend loyalty by ufing arguments to prove that it was againft the royal prerogative, for the parliament to entrench upon the king's right of calling and diffolving of parliaments : as if there were a prerogative in the crown, to chufe whether ever a parliament fhould affemble, or no. I would defire no more, if I were a prince, to make me grand feignior. Soon after this laft act, the king, by reafon of his wars with France and Scotland, and other great affairs, was forced fometimes to end his parliaments abruptly, and leave bufinefs undone ; (and this not out of court-tricks, which were then unknown :) which produced another act not long after, by which it was provided ; that no parliament fhould be difmift, till all the petitions were anfwered. That is, in the language of thofe times, till all
the

the bills (which were then ftiled petitions) were finifhed.

Doct. Pray, fir, give me a little account of this laft act you fpeak of; for I have heard in difcourfe from many lawyers, that they believe there is no fuch.

Eng. Gent. Truly, fir, I fhall confefs to you, that I do not find this law in any of our printed ftatute-books. But that which firft gave me the knowledge of it, was what was faid about three years ago in the houfe of commons, by a worthy and learned gentleman, who undertook to produce the record in the reign of Richard the fecond: and fince, I have queftioned many learned counfellors about it, who tell me there is fuch a one: and one of them, who is counted a prerogative lawyer, faid it was fo; but that the act was made in factious times. Befides, I think it will be granted, that for fome time after, (and particularly in the reigns of Henry the fourth, Henry the fifth, and Henry the fixth) is was ufual for a proclamation to be made in Weftminfter-hall, before the end of every feffion: That all thofe that had any matter to prefent to the parliament, fhould bring it in before fuch a day;

day; for otherwife, the parliament at that day fhould determine. But if there were nothing at all of this, nor any record extant concerning it; yet I muft believe that it is fo by the fundamental law of this government, which muft be lame and imperfect without it. For it is all one to have no parliaments at all but when the prince pleafes, and to allow a power in him to difmifs them when he will; that is, when they refufe to do what he will. So that if there be no ftatute, it is certainly becaufe our wife anceftors thought there needed none, but that by the very effence and conftitution of the government it is provided for. And this we may call (if you had rather have it fo) the common law; which is of as much value (if not more) than any ftatute, and of which all our good acts of parliament, and *Magna Charta* itfelf, is but declaratory. So that your objection is fufficiently anfwered in this, that though the king is intrufted with the formal part of fummoning and pronouncing the diffolution of parliaments, which is done by his writ; yet the laws (which oblige him as well as us) have determin'd, how and when he

fhall

shall do it: which is enough to shew, that the king's share in the soveraignty, (that is, in the parliament,) is cut out to him by the law, and not left at his disposal. Now I come to the king's part in the intervals of parliament.

Noble Ven. Sir, before you do so, pray tell us what other prerogatives the king enjoys in the government; for otherwise, I who am a Venetian, may be apt to think that our Doge, who is call'd our prince, may have as much power as yours.

Eng. Gent. I am in a fine condition amongst you, with my politicks: the doctor tells me, I have made the king absolute; and now you tell me, I have made him a Doge of Venice. But when your prince has power to dispose of the publick revenue; to name all officers ecclesiastical and civil, that are of trust and profit in the kingdom; and to dispose absolutely of the whole militia, by sea, and land; then we will allow him to be like ours, who has all these powers.

Doct. Well, you puzzle me extreamly! For when you had asserted the king's power to the heighth, in calling and dissolving

par-

parliaments, you gave me such satisfaction, and shewed me wherein the law had provided that this vast prerogative could not hurt the people, that I was fully satisfied; and had not a word to say: now you come about again, and place in the crown such a power, which in my judgment is inconsistent with our liberty.

Eng. Gen. Sir, I suppose you mean chiefly the power of the militia; which was, I must confess, doubtful, before a late statute declar'd it to be in the king. For our government hath made no other disposal of the militia, than what was natural; *viz.* that the peers in their several counties, or jurisdictions, had the power of calling together their vassals: either armed for the wars, or only so as to cause the law to be executed by serving writs; and in case of resistance, giving possession: which lords amongst their own tenants did then perform the two several offices of lord lieutenant, and sheriff; which latter was but the earl's deputy, as by his title of *vice-comes* does appear. But this latter being of daily necessity; and justice itself (that is, the lives, liberties and estates of all the people in that county)

county) depending upon it; when the greatness of the peers decay'd, (of which we
shall have occasion to speak hereafter,) the
electing of sheriff was referred to the county-
court: where it continued, till it was placed
where it now is by a statute. For the other
part of the militia; which is, the arming
the people for war, it was *de facto* exercised
by commission from the king, to a lord-
lieutenant (as an image of the natural lord)
and other deputies: and it was tacitly consented to, though it were never settled by
statute, (as I said before,) till his majesty's
happy restauration. But to answer you I
shall say, that whatever powers are in the
crown, whether by statute or by old pre-
scription, they are, and must be understood
to be intrusted in the prince for the preservation of the government, and for the safety
and interest of the people: and when either
the militia, which is given him for the execution and support of the law, shall be imploy'd by him to subvert it, (as in the
case of ship-money it was;) or the treasure
shall be misapply'd, and made the revenue
of courtiers and sycophants, (as in the time
of Edward the second;) or worthless or
wicked

wicked people shall be put into the greatest
places, (as in the reign of Richard the second: (in this case, though the prince here
cannot be questionable for it, (as the kings
were in Sparta, and your doges I believe
would be ;) yet it is a great violation of the
trust reposed in him by the government :
and a making that power, which is given
him by law, unlawful in the execution. And
the frequent examples of justice inflicted in
parliament upon the king's ministers, for
abusing the royal power, shew plainly that
such authority is not left in his hands to use
as he pleases. Nay, there have befallen sad
troubles and dangers to some of these princes
themselves, who have abused their power
to the prejudice of the subjects ; which although they are no way justifiable, yet
may serve for an instruction to princes, and
an example not to hearken to ruinous counsels : for men when they are enraged do not
always consider justice, or religion ; passion
being as natural to man as reason and virtue : which was the opinion of divine Machiavil. To answer you then, I say, that
though we do allow such powers in the
king ; yet since they are given him for edi-

G
fication

fication and not deftruction, and cannot be abufed without great danger to his minifters, and even to himfelf: we may hope that they can never be abufed but in a broken government. And if ours be fo (as we fhall fee anon) the fault of the ill execution of our laws is not to be imputed either to the prince or his minifters; excepting that the latter may be, as we faid before, juftly punifhable for not advifing the prince to confent to the mending the frame: of which we fhall talk more hereafter. But in the mean time I will come to the king's other prerogatives: as having all royal mines; the being ferv'd firft before other creditors where money is due to him; and to have a fpeedier and eafier way than his fubjects, to recover his debts and his rents; *&c.* But to fay all in one word, when there arifes any doubt whether any thing be the king's prerogative or no, this is the way of deciding it: *viz.* To confider whether it be for the good and protection of the people, that the king have fuch a power; for the definition of prerogative is a confiderable part of the common-law, by which power is put into the prince for the prefervation

of

of his people. And if be not for the good
of his subjects, it is not prerogative, nor
law; for our prince has no authority of his
own, but what was first intrusted in him by
the government, of which he is head : nor
is it to be imagined that they would give him
more power than what was necessary to govern them. For example, the power of
pardoning criminals condemned, is of such
use to the lives and estates of the people,
that without it many would be exposed to
die unjustly. As lately a poor gentleman,
who by means of the harangue of a strep-
itous lawyer was found guilty of murder,
for a man he never kill'd ; or if he had, the
fact had been but man-slaughter ; and he
had been inevitably murdered himself, if his
majesty had not been graciously pleased to
extend his royal mercy to him : as he did
likewise vouchsafe to do to a gentleman con-
victed for speaking words he never utter'd ;
or if he had spoken them, they were but
foolishly not maliciously spoken. On the
other side, if a controversy should arise, as
it did in the beginning of the last parliament, between the house of commons and
the prerogative lawyers, about the choice

of

of their speaker; these latter having interested his majesty in the contest, and made him, by consequence, disoblige, *in limine*, a very loyal, and a very worthy parliament: and for what? For a question, which if you will decide it the right way, will be none; for setting aside the presidents, and the history when the crown first pretended to any share in the choice of a speaker, (which argument was very well handled by some of the learned patriots then;) I would have leave to ask, what man can shew, and what reason can be alledged, why the protection and welfare of the people should require that a prerogative should be in the prince to chuse the mouth of the house of commons; when there is no particular person in his whole dominion that would not think it against his interest, if the government had given the king power to nominate his bayliff, his attorney, or his referree in any arbitration? Certainly there can be no advantage either to the soveraign or his subjects, that the person whose office it is to put their deliberations into fitting words, and express all their

requests

requefts to his majefty, fhould not be entirely in their own election and appoint-
ment : which there is the more reafon for
too, becaufe the fpeakers for many years
paft have received inftructions from the
court ; and have broken the privileges of
the houfe, by revealing their debates, adjourning them without a vote ; and committed many other mifdemeanours, by
which they have begotten an ill underftanding between the king and his houfe of
commons, to the infinite prejudice both of
his majefty's affairs and his people. Since
I have given this rule to judge prerogative
by, I fhall fay no more of it : for as to
what concerns the king's office in the intervals of parliament, it is wholly mini-
fterial ; and is barely to put in execution
the common law, and the ftatutes made by
the foveraign power (that is, by himfelf and
the parliament) without varying one tittle ;
or fufpending, abrogating, or neglecting
the execution of any act whatfoever : and
to this he is folemnly fworn at his corona-
tion. And all his power in this behalf is in
him by common law ; which is reafon it

self :

felf: written as well in the hearts of rational men, as in the lawyers books.

Noble Ven. Sir, I have heard much talk of the king's negative voice in parliaments; which in my opinion is as much as a power to fruftrate, when he pleafes, all the endeavours and labours of his people, and to prevent any good that might accrue to the kingdom by having the right to meet in parliament : for certainly, if we in Venice had placed any fuch prerogative in our duke, or in any of our magiftracies, we could not call our felves a free people.

Eng. Gent. Sir, I can anfwer you, as I did before : that if our kings have fuch a power, it ought to be ufed according to the true and genuine intent of the government ; that is, for the prefervation and intereft of the people ; and not for the difappointing the counfels of a parliament towards reforming grievances, and making provifion : for the future execution of the laws. And whenever it is applied to fruftrate thofe ends, it is a violation of right, and infringment of the king's coronation-oath ; in which there is this claufe,

tha

that he fhall *confirmare confuetudines* (which, in the Latin of thofe times, is *leges)* *quas vulgus elegerit.* I know fome criticks, who are rather grammarians than lawyers, have made a diftinction between *elegerim* and *elegero* : and will have it, that the king fwears to fuch laws as the people *fhall have chofen* : and not to thofe they *fhall chufe.* But in my opinion, if that claufe had been intended only to oblige the king to execute the laws made already, it might have been better expreft by *fervare confuetudines*, than by *confirmare confuetudines* ; befides that he is by another claufe in the fame oath fworn to execute all the laws. But I fhall leave this controverfy undecided : thofe who have a defire to fee more of it, may look into thofe quarreling declarations *pro* and *con* about this matter, which preceded our unhappy civil wars. This is certain, that there are not to be found any ftatutes that have paffed, without being prefented to his majefty, or to fome commiffioned by him ; but whether fuch addreffes were intended for refpect and honour to his majefty, as the fpeaker of the houfe of commons and the lord mayor of London are brought to him,

him, I leave to the learned to difcourfe.
Only thus much we may affirm ; that there
never were yet any parliamentary requefts,
which did highly concern the publick, prefented to any king and by him refufed, but
fuch denials did produce very difmal effects :
as may be feen in our hiftories ancient
and late : it being certain, that both the
barons wars, and our laft difmal combuftions, proceeded from no other caufe than
the denial of the princes then reigning to
confent to the defires of the ftates of the
kingdom. And fuch hath been the wifdom and goodnefs of our prefent gracious
prince; that in twenty years, and fome-
what more (for which time we have enjoyed him, fince his happy reftauration) he hath
not exercis'd his negative voice towards
more than one publick bill ; and that too,
was to have continued in force (if it had
paffed into an act) but for fix weeks ; being
for raifing the militia for fo long time : and
as for the private bills, which are matters
of meer grace, it is unreafonable his majefty fhould be refufed that right that every
Englifhman enjoys, which is not to be
obliged to difpenfe his favours but where
he

he pleafes. But for this point of the negative vote; it is poffible that when we come to difcourfe of the cure of our political diftemper, fome of you will propofe the clearing and explanation of this matter, and of all others which may concern the king's power and the people's rights.

Noble Ven. But pray, fir, have not the houfe of peers a negative voice in all bills? How come they not to be obliged to ufe it for the publick good?

Eng. Gent. So they are, no doubt; and the commons too: but there is a vaft difference between a deliberative vote, which the peers have with their negative; and that in the crown, to blaft all without deliberating. The peers are co-ordinate with the commons in prefenting and hammering of laws; and may fend bills down to them, as well as receive any from them; excepting in matters wherein the people are to be taxed. And in this our government imitates the beft and moft perfect commonwealths that ever were: where the fenate affifted in the making of laws; and by their wifdom and dexterity, polifht, fil'd, and made ready things for the more populous affemblies: and fometimes

times

times by their gravity and moderation, reduced the people to a calmer state; and by their authority and credit stem'd the tide, and made the waters quiet, giving the people time to come to themselves. And therefore if we had no such peerage now, upon the old conftitution ; yet we fhould be neceffitated to make an artificial peerage or fenate in ftead of it. Which may affure our prefent lords, that though their dependences and power are gone, yet we cannot be without them : and that they have no need to fear an annihilation by our reformation, as they fuffered in the late mad times. But I fhall fpeak a word of the people's rights ; and then fhew how this brave and excellent government of England came to decay.

The people by the fundamental laws, (that is, by the conftitution of the government of England) have entire freedom in their lives, properties, and their perfons : neither of which can in the leaft fuffer, but according to the laws already made ; or to be made hereafter in parliament, and duly publifht. And to prevent any oppreffion that might happen in the execution of thefe good

good laws, (which are our birth-right) all trials muſt be by twelve men of our e-quals, and of our neighbourhood. Theſe in all civil cauſes judge abſolutely, and de-cide the matter of fact, upon which the matter of law depends : but if where mat-ter of law is in queſtion, theſe twelve men ſhall refuſe to find a ſpecial verdict at the direction of the court, the judge cannot controul it ; but their verdict muſt be re-corded. But of theſe matters, as alſo of demurrers, writs of error, and arreſts of judgment, &c. I have diſcours'd to this gentleman (who is a ſtranger) before now ; neither do's the underſtanding of the execu-tion of our municipal laws at all belong to this diſcourſe. Only it is to be noted, that theſe juries, or twelve men, in all trials or cauſes which are criminal, have ab-ſolute power, both as to matter of law, and fact, (except the party by demurrer con-feſs the matter of fact, and take it out of their hands.) And the firſt queſtion the officer aſks the foreman, when they all come in to deliver their verdict, is this ; is he guilty in manner and form as he is indicted, or not guilty ?. Which ſhews plain-

ly,

ly, that they are to examine and judge, as
well whether, and how far the fact committed is criminal, as whether the person
charged hath committed that fact. But
though by the corruption of these times
(the infallible consequences of a broken
frame of government) this office of the
juries and right of Englishmen have been
of late question'd, yet it hath been strong-
ly and effectually vindicated by a learned
author of late, to whom I refer you for
more of this matter. I shall say no more
of the rights of the people, but this one
thing; that neither the king, nor any by
authority from him, hath any the least
power or jurisdiction over any Englishman,
but what the law gives them : and that although all commissions and writs go out in
the king's name, yet his majesty hath no
right to issue out any writ (with advice of
his council, or otherwise) excepting what
come out of his courts ; nor to alter any
clause in a writ, or add any thing to it.
And if any person shall be so wicked as to
do any injustice to the life, liberty, or estate
of any Englishman, by any private command of the prince, the person aggrieved,

or

or his next of kin (if he be affaffinated) shall have the same remedy against the offender, as he ought to have had by the good laws of this land, if there had been no such command given : which would be absolutely void and null, and understood not to proceed from that royal and lawful power which is vested in his majesty, for the execution of justice and the protection of his people.

Doct. Now I see you have done with all the government of England ; pray before you proceed to the decay of it, let me ask you what you think of the Chancery : whether you do not believe it a solecism in the politicks to have such a court amongst a free people. What good will Magna Charta, the petition of right, or St. Edward's laws do us to defend our property, if it must be entirely subjected to the arbitrary disposal of one man, whenever any impertinent or petulant person shall put in a bill against you ? How inconsistent is this tribunal with all that hath been said in defence of our rights, or can be said ? Suppose the prince should, in time to come, so little respect his own honour and the interest

2

tereft of his people, as to place a covetous or revengeful perfon in that great judicatory; what remedy have we againft the corruption of regifters, who make what orders they pleafe; or againft the whole hierarchy of knavifh clerks? Whilft not only the punifhing and reforming mifdemeanours depend upon him, who may without controul be the moft guilty himfelf; but that all the laws of England ftand there arraigned before him, and may be condemned when he pleafes. Is there, or ever was there any fuch tribunal in the world before, in any country?

Eng. Gent. Doctor, I find you have had a fuit in chancery: but I do not intend to contradict or blame your orthodox zeal in this point. This court is one of thofe buildings that cannot be repaired, but muft be demolifhed. I could inform you how excellently matters of equity are adminiftred in other countries; and this worthy gentleman could tell you of the venerable Quarantzia's in his city, where the law as well as the fact, is at the bar, and fubject to the judges, and yet no complaint made or grievance fuffered. But this is not a place for

it,

it, this is but the fuperſtructure : we muſt ſettle the foundation firſt. Every thing elſe is as much out of order as this : trade is gone ; ſuits are endleſs ; and nothing a-mongſt us harmonious. But all will come right when our government is mend-ed ; and never before, though our judges were all angels. This is the *primum quæ-rite* ; when you have this, all other things ſhall be added unto you. When that is done, neither the chancery (which is grown up to this ſince our anceſtors time) nor the ſpiritual courts, nor the cheats in trade, nor any other abuſes, no not the giant po-pery it ſelf, ſhall ever be able to ſtand be-fore a parliament ; no more than one of us can live, like a ſalamander, in the fire.

Noble Ven. Therefore, ſir, pray let us come now to the decay of your govern-ment ; that we may come the ſooner to the happy reſtauration.

Eng. Gent. This harmonious government of England being founded as has been ſaid upon property, it was impoſſible it ſhould be ſhaken ſo long as property remain'd where it was placed : for if, when the an-cient owners the Britains fled into the mountains,

tains, and left their lands to the invaders
(who divided them, as is above related)
they had made an Agrarian law to fix it ;
then our government, and by confequence
our happinefs, had been for aught we know
immortal. For our conftitution, as it was
really a mixture of the three, (which are
Monarchy, Ariftocracy, and Democracy,
as has been faid) fo the weight and predo-
minancy remained in the Optimacy ; who
poffeffed nine parts in ten of the lands, and
the prince but about a tenth part. In this
I count all the peoples fhares to the peers,
and therefore do not trouble myfelf to enquire what proportion was allotted to them ;
for although they had an hereditary right in
their lands, yet it was fo clog'd with tenures and fervices, that they depended, as to
publick matters, wholly on their lords :
who by them could ferve the king in his
wars ; and in time of peace, by leading the
people to what they pleafed, could keep the
royal power within its due bounds ; and alfo hinder and prevent the people, from invading the rights of the crown. So that
they were the bulwarks of the government ;
which in effect was much more an Ariftocracy,

tracy, than either a Monarchy or Democracy : and in all governments, where property is mixt, the administration is so too ; and that part which hath the greater share in the lands, will have it too in the jurisdiction. And so in commonwealths, the senate or the people have more or less power, as they have more or fewer possessions, as was most visible in Rome, where in the beginning, the Patricii could hardly bring the people to any thing; but afterwards, when the Asiatick conquests had inricht the nobility to that degree, that they were able to purchase a great part of the lands in Italy, the people were all their clients, and easily brought even to cut the throats of their redeemers the Gracchi, who had carried a law for restoring them their lands. But enough of this before. I will not trouble my self, nor you, to search into the particular causes of this change which has been made in the possessions here in England ; but it is visible that the fortieth part of the lands which were at the beginning in the hands of the peers and church, is not there now : besides that not only all villanage is long since abolished, but the other
tenures

tenures are so altered and qualified, that they signifie nothing towards making the yeomanry depend upon the lords. The consequence is : that the natural part of our government, which is power, is by means of property in the hands of the people; whilst the artificial part, or the parchment in which the form of government is written, remains the same. Now art is a very good servant and help to nature, but very weak and inconsiderable, when she opposes her, and fights with her ; it would be a very *impar congressus*, between parchment and power. This alone is the cause of all the disorder you heard of, and now see in England ; and of which every man gives a reason according to his own fancy, whilst few hit the right cause. Some impute all to the decay of trade ; others to the growth of popery : which are both great calamities, but they are effects, and not causes. And if in private families there were the same causes, there would be the same effects : suppose now you had five or six thousand pounds a year, (as it is probable you have,) and keep forty servants ; and at length by your neglect, and the industry and thrift

of

of your domefticks, you fell one thoufand
to your fteward, another to your clerk of
the kitchen, another to your bailiff, till all
were gone : can you believe that thefe fervants, when they had fo good eftates of their
own, and you nothing left to give them,
would continue to live with you, and to do
their fervice as before ? It is juft fo with a
whole kingdom. In our anceftors times,
moft of the members of our houfe of commons thought it an honour to retain to
fome great lord, and to wear his blue coat :
and when they had made up their lord's
train, and waited upon him from his own
houfe to the lords houfe, and made a lane
for him to enter, and departed to fit themfelves in the lower houfe of parliament, as
it was then (and very juftly) called ; can
you think that any thing could pafs in fuch
a parliament, that was not ordered by
the lords ? Befides, thefe lords were the
king's great council in the intervals of parliaments, and were called to advife of peace
and war ; and the latter was feldom made
without the confent of the major part : if it
were, they would not fend their tenants ;
which

which was all the militia of England, befides the king's tenth part. Can it be believed, that in thofe days the commons
fhould diflike any thing the lords did in the
intervals, or that they would have difputed
their right to receive appeals from courts of
equity, if they had pretended to it in thofe
days, or to mend money-bills ? And what
is the reafon, but becaufe the lords themfelves at that time reprefented all their te-
ants (that is, all the people) in fome fort ?
And although the houfe of commons did
affemble to prefent their grievances, yet all
great affairs of high importance concerning
the government, were tranfacted by the
lords ; and the war which was made to preferve it, was called the barons wars, not the
war of both houfes : for although in anci-
enter times the word baron was taken in a
larger fenfe, and comprehended the Francklins or Freemen ; yet who reads any hiftory
of that war, fhall not find that any mention is made of the concurrence of any affembly of fuch men : but that Simon Mon-
ford earl of Leicefter, and others of the
great ones, did by their power and intereft
manage that conteft. Now if this property
which

which is gone out of the peerage into
the commons, had paffed into the king's
hands, as it did in Egypt in the time of
Jofeph ; as was before faid, the prince had
had a very eafy and peaceable reign over
his own vaffals : and might either have refufed, juftly, to have affembled the parliament any more ; or if he had pleafed to do
it, might have for ever managed it as he
thought fit. But our princes have wanted
a Jofeph : that is, a wife counfellor ; and
inftead of faving their revenue, which was
very great and their expences fmall ; and
buying in thofe purchafes, which the vaft
expences and luxury of the lords made ready
for them ; they have alienated their own
inheritance. So that now the crown-lands,
that is, the publick patrimony, is come to
make up the intereft of the commons :
whilft the king muft have a precarious revenue out of the peoples purfes ; and be
beholden to the parliament for his bread in
time of peace : whereas the kings their predeceffors never afked aid of his fubjects, but
in time of war and invafion. And this
alone (though there were no other decay in
government) is enough to make the king
depend

depend upon his people : which is no very good condition for a monarchy.

Noble Ven. But how comes it to pass that other neighbouring countries are in so settled a state in respect of England ? does their property remain the same it was, or is it come into the hands of the prince ? You know you were pleased to admit, that we should ask you, *en passant*, something of other countries.

Eng. Gen. Sir, I thank you for it, and shall endeavour to satisfy you. I shall say nothing of the small princes of Germany ; who keep in a great measure their ancient bounds, both of government and property : and if their princes now and then exceed their part ; yet it is in time of troubles and war, and things return into their right chanel of assembling the several states, which are yet in being every where. But Germany lying so exposed to the invasion of the Turks on the one side, and of the French on the other ; and having ever had enough to do to defend their several liberties against the encroachments of the house of Austria (in which the imperial dignity is become in some sort hereditary) if there

had

had been fomething of extraordinary power exercifed of late years, I can fay *inter arma filent leges :* but befides their own particular ftates, they have the diet of the empire, which never fails to mediate and compofe things ; if there be any great oppreffion ufed by princes to their fubjects, or from one prince or ftate to another. I fhall therefore confine myfelf to the three great kingdoms, France, Spain, and Poland : for as to Denmark and Sweden, the firft hath lately chang'd its government, and not only made the monarchy hereditary, which was before elective ; but has pull'd down the nobility, and given their power to the prince : which how it will fucceed, time will fhew. Sweden remains in point of conftitution, and property, exactly as it did anciently ; and is a well-governed kingdom. The firft of the other three, is France ; of which I have fpoken before, and fhall only add : that though it be very true, that there is property in France, and yet the government is defpotical at this prefent ; yet it is one of thofe violent ftates, which the Grecians called tyrannies. For if a lawful prince (that is, one who being

2

fo

so by law, and sworn to rule according to it) breaks his oaths and his bonds, and reigns arbitrarily, he becomes a tyrant and an usurper, as to so much as he assumes more than the constitution hath given him : and such a government, being as I said violent, and not natural, but contrary to the interest of the people, cannot be lasting when the adventitious props which support it fail ; and whilst it does endure, must be very uneasy both to prince and people : the first being necessitated to use continual oppression, and the latter to suffer it.

Doct. You are pleased to talk of the oppression of the people under the king of France, and for that reason, call it a violent government ; when, if I remember, you did once to day extol the monarchy of the Turks for well-founded and natural : are not the people in that empire as much oppressed as in France ?

Eng. Gent. By no means : unless you will call it oppression for the grand seignior to feed all his people out of the product of his own lands : and though they serve him for it, yet that does not alter the case ; for if you set poor men to work and pay them

for

for it, are you a tyrant? Or rather, are not you a good commonwealths-man, by helping thofe to live who have no other way of doing it but by their labour? But the king of France knowing that his people have, and ought to have property; and that he has no right to their poffeffions; yet takes what he pleafes from them, without their confent, and contrary to law: fo that when he fets them on work he pays them what he pleafes, and that he levies out of their own eftates. I do not affirm that there is no government in the world, but where rule is founded in property; but I fay there is no natural fixed government, but where it is fo. And when it is otherwife, the people are perpetually complaining, and the king in perpetual anxiety; always in fear of his fubjects, and feeking new ways to fecure himfelf: God having been fo merciful to mankind, that he hath made nothing fafe for princes, but what is juft and honeft.

Noble Ven. But you were faying juft now, that this prefent conftitution in France will fall when the props fail; we in Italy, who live in perpetual fear of the

great-

greatnefs of that kingdom, would be glad to hear fomething of the decaying of thofe props : what are they, I befeech you ?

Eng. Gent. The firft is the greatnefs of the prefent king : whofe heroick actions and wifdom has extinguifhed envy in all his neighbour-princes, and kindled fear ; and brought him to be above all poffibility of control at home : not only becaufe his fubjects fear his courage, but becaufe they have his virtue in admiration ; and amidft all their miferies cannot chufe but have fomething of rejoycing, to fee how high he hath mounted the empire and honour of their nation. The next prop, is the change of their ancient conftitution ; in the time of Charles the feventh, by confent : for about that time the country being fo wafted by the invafion and excurfions of the Englifh, the ftates, then affembled, petitioned the king that he would give them leave to go home, and difpofe of affairs himfelf ; and order the government for the future, as he thought fit. Upon this, his fucceffor Lewis the eleventh, being a crafty prince, took an occafion to call the ftates no more ; but to fupply them with an *Affemblé des notables :*

notables : which were certain men of his own nomination, like Barbone's parliament here, but that they were of better quality. These in succeeding reigns, (being the best men of the kingdom,) grew troublesome and intractable; so that for some years the edicts have been verified, (that is, in our language, bills have been passed) in the grand chamber of the parliament at Paris, commonly called the *Chambre d' audience* : who lately, (and since the imprisonment of president Brousselles, and others, during this king's minority,) have never refused or scrupled any edicts whatsoever. Now whenever this great king dies ; and the states of the kingdom are restored ; these two great props of arbitrary power are taken away. Besides these two, the constitution of the government of France it self, is somewhat better fitted than ours, to permit extraordinary power in the prince. For the whole people there possessing lands are gentlemen ; (that is, infinitely the greater part ;) which was the reason why in their assembly of estates, the deputies of the provinces (which we call here knights of the shire) were chosen by, and out of the gentry :

and

and fate with the peers in the fame chamber, as reprefenting the gentry only, called *Petite nobleſſe*. Whereas our knights here (whatever their blood is) are chofen by commoners ; and are commoners : our laws and government taking no notice of any nobility, but the perfons of the peers ; whofe fons are likewife commoners, even their eldeſt, whilſt their fathers live. Now gentry are ever more tractable by a prince, than a wealthy and numerous commonalty ; out of which our gentry (at leaſt thofe we call fo) are raifed from time to time : for whenever either a merchant, lawyer, tradefman, grafier, farmer, or any other gets fuch an eſtate, as that he or his fon can live upon his lands without exercifing of any other calling, he becomes a gentleman. I do not fay, but that we have men very nobly defcended amongſt thefe ; but they have no preheminence, or diftinction, by the laws or government. Befides this, the gentry in France are very needy, and very numerous : the reafon of which is, that the elder brother in moſt parts of that kingdom hath no more fhare in the divifion of the paternal eſtate than the cadets or younger brothers ;

excepting

excepting the principal houfe, with the or-
chards and gardens about it : which they
call *Vol de Chappon*, as who fhould fay as
far as a capon can fly at once. This houfe
gives him the title his father had, who was
called feignior, or baron, or count of that
place ; which if he fells, he parts with his
baronfhip : and for aught I know becomes
in time *roturier*, or ignoble. This practice
divides the lands into fo many fmall parcels,
that the poffeffors of them being noble, and
having little to maintain their nobility, are
fain to feek their fortune ; which they can
find no where fo well as at the court ; and
fo become the king's fervants and foldiers ;
for they are generally couragious, bold, and
of a good mien. None of thefe can ever
advance themfelves but by their defert ;
which makes them hazard themfelves very
defperately : by which means great numbers of them are kill'd ; and the reft come
in time to be great officers, and live fplen-
didly upon the king's purfe : who is likewife very liberal to them ; and according
to their refpective merits, gives them often,
in the beginning of a campagne, a confiderable fum to furnifh out their equipage.

Thefe

These are a great prop to the regal power : it being their interest to support it ; lest their gain should cease, and they be reduced to be poor *Provinciaux*, that is country-gentlemen, again. Whereas if they had such estates as our country-gentry have, they would desire to be at home at their ease ; whilst these (having ten times as much from the king as their own estates can yield them, which supply must fail if the king's revenue were reduced) are perpetually engaged to make good all exorbitances.

Doct. This is a kind of governing by property too : and it puts me in mind of a gentleman of good estate in our country, who took a tenant's son of his to be his servant ; whose father not long after dying, left him a living of about ten pound a year. The young man's friends came to him, and asked him why he would serve, now he had an estate of his own able to maintain him ? His answer was, that his own lands would yield him but a third part of what his service was worth to him in all : besides, that he lived a pleasant life ; wore good cloaths ; kept good company ; and had the

con-

conversation of very pretty maids, that were his fellow-servants ; which made him very well digest the name of being a servant.

Eng. Gent. This is the very case ; but yet service, in both these cases, is no inheritance. And when there comes a peaceable king in France who will let his neighbours be quiet, or one that is covetous ; these fine gentlemen will lose their employments, and their king this prop : and the rather, because these gentlemen do not depend (as was said before) in any kind upon the great lords whose standing interest is at court ; and so cannot in a change, be by them carried over to advance the court-designs, against their own good and that of their country. And thus much is sufficient to be said concerning France. As for Spain ; I believe there is no country (excepting Sweden) in Christendom, where the property has remained so intirely the same it was at the beginning : and the reason is, the great and strict care that is taken to hinder the lands from passing out of the old owners hands. For except it be by marriages, no man can acquire another

man's

man's eftate ; nor can any Grandee, or Ti-
tulador, or any other Hidalgo there, alien-
ate or engage his paternal or maternal
eftate, otherwife than for his life ; nor can
alter tenures, or extinguifh fervices, or dif-
member mannors : for to this the prince's
confent muft be had, which he never gives
till the matter be debated in the *confejo de
camera* : which is no *junta*, or fecret *confejo de guerras* ; but one wherein the great
men of the kingdom intervene, and wherein the great matters concerning the prefervation of the government are tranfacted,
not relating to foreign provinces or governments, but to the kingdom of Caftile and
Leon ; of which only I fpeak now. It is
true, there have been one or two excepti-
ons againft this fevere rule, fince the great
calamities of Spain ; and two great lordfhips have been fold, the Marquifate *del
Monaftero* to an *affentifta* Genoefe, and another to *Sebaftian Cortiza* a Portuguefe of
the fame profeffion : but both thefe have
bought the entire lordfhips, without cur-
tailing or altering the condition in which
thefe two great eftates were before ; and
notwithftanding, this hath caufed fo much
repining

repining amongſt the natural Godos (as the Caſtilians call themſelves ſtill for glory) that I believe this will never be drawn into an example hereafter. Now the property remaining the ſame, the government doth ſo too ; and the king's domeſtick government, over his natural Spaniards, is very gentle, whatever it be in his conquer'd provinces : and the kings there have very great advantages of keeping their great men (by whom they govern) in good temper, by reaſon of the great governments they have to beſtow upon them, both in Europe and the Indies ; which changing every three years, go in an age through all the grandees, which are not very numerous. Beſides, Caſtile having been in the time of king Roderigo over-run and conquered by the Moors (who governed there deſpotically, ſome hundreds of years, before it could be recovered again by the old inhabitants who fled to the mountains ;) when they were at length driven out, the count of Caſtile found a tax ſet upon all commodities whatſoever by the Moors in their reign, called Alcaval ; which was an eaſie matter to get continued, when their old government

H 5 was

was reſtored, by the Cortes or States : and ſo it has continued ever ſince, as the exciſe has done here ; which being impoſed by them who drove and kept out the king, does now ſince his happy reſtauration remain a revenue of the crown. This Alcaval, or exciſe, is a very great revenue ; and ſo prevented, for ſome time, the neceſſities of the crown, and made the prince have the leſs need of aſking relief of his people, the ordinary cauſe of diſguſt : ſo that the Cortes, or aſſembly of the States, has had little to do of late ; though they are duly aſſembled every year, but ſeldom contradict what is deſired by the prince ; for there are no greater idolaters of their monarch in the world than the Caſtilians are, nor who drink deeper of the cup of loyalty. So that in ſhort the government in Spain is, as ours was in queen Elizabeth's time ; or in the firſt year after his now majeſty's return ; when the parliament for a time complimented the prince, who had by that means both his own power and the peoples : which days I hope to ſee again, upon a better and more laſting foundation. But before I leave Spain,

3 I

I muſt ſay a word of the kingdom of Arragon ;
which has not at all times had ſo quiet a ſtate
of their monarchy, as Caſtile hath enjoyed.
For after many combuſtions which happened there concerning there Fueros and Privilegios, which are their fundamental laws ;
the king one day coming to his ſeat in parliament, and making his demands as was
uſual, they told him that they had a requeſt
to make to him firſt : and he withdraw-
ing thereupon, (for he had no right of ſit-
ing there to hear their debates) they fell
into diſcourſe how to make their government ſubſiſt againſt the encroachments of
the prince upon them ; and went very high
in their debates, which could not chuſe but
come to the king's ear, who walked in a
gallery in the ſame palace to expect the
iſſue : and being in great paſſion, was ſeen
to draw out his dagger very often, and
thruſt it again into the ſheath ; and heard
to ſay, *ſangre ha de coſtar !* Which coming to the knowledge of the eſtates, they
left off the debate ; and ſent ſome of their
number to him, to know what blood it
ſhould coſt, and whether he meant to murder any body. He drew out his dagger
again,

again, and pointing it to his breast, he said, *sangre de reys*; leaving them in doubt, whether he meant that his subjects would kill him, or that he would do it himself. However, that parliament ended very peaceably: and a famous settlement was there and then made, by which a great person was to be chosen every parliament, who should be as it were an umpire between the king and his people; for the execution of the laws, and the preservation of their government, their Fueros and Privilegios; which are their courts of justice, and their charters. This officer was called, *el Justicia d'Arragon*; and his duty was to call together the whole power of the kingdom, whenever any of the aforesaid rights were by open force violated or invaded, and to admonish the king whenever he heard of any clandestine counsels among them to that effect. It was likewise made treason, for any person of what quallity soever, to refuse to repair upon due summons to any place where this Justicia should erect his standard; or to withdraw himself without leave; much more, to betray him, or to revolt from him. Besides, in this Cortes or

parlia-

parliament, the old oath which at the first
foundation of their state was ordered to be
taken by the king at his admittance, was
again revived ; which is in these words :
*nos que valemos tanto come vos, y podemos mas,
vos eligimos nuestro reyes, conque vos guar-
deys nuestros fueros y privilegios : y si no, no.*
That is ; " *We who are as good as you, and*
" *more powerful, do chuse you our king ; up-*
" *on condition that you preserve our rights*
" *and privileges : and otherwise, we do not*
" *chuse you.* " Notwithstanding all this,
Philip the second, being both king of
Castile and Arragon, pick'd a quarrel with
the latter, by demanding his secretary An-
tonio Perez, who fled from the king's dif-
pleasure thither, being his own country ;
and they refusing to deliver him (it being
expresly contrary to a law of Arragon,
that a subject of that kingdom should be
against his will carried to be tryed elsewhere :) the king took that occasion, to invade them with the forces of his kingdom of
Castile, (who had ever been rivals and enemies to the Arragonefes ;) and they, to defend themselves under their Justicia, who
did his part faithfully and couragioufly ; but

the Caſtilians being old ſoldiers, and thoſe of Arragon but county-troops, the former prevailed : and ſo this kingdom, in getting that of Caſtile by a marriage but an age before, loſt its own liberty and government ; for it is ſince made a province and governed by a vice-roy from Madrid, although they keep up the formality of their Cortes ſtill.

Doɛt. No man living that knew the hatred and hoſtility that ever was between the Engliſh and Scots, could have imagined in the years 1639 and 1640, (when our king was with great armies of Engliſh upon the frontiers of Scotland, ready to invade that kingdom) that this nation would not have aſſiſted, to have brought them under ; but it proved otherwiſe.

Eng. Gent. It may be, they feared, when Scotland was reduced to ſlavery, and the province pacified and forces kept up there, ſuch forces and greater might have been imployed here to reduce us into the ſame condition ; an apprehenſion, which at this time ſticks with many of the common people, and helps to fill up the meaſure of our fears and diſtractions. But the viſible reaſon,

son, why the English were not at that time very forward to oppress their neighbours, was the confideration that they were to be invaded for refusing to receive from hence certain innovations in matters of religion, and the worship of God, which had not long before been introduced here; and therefore the people of this kingdom were unwilling to perpetuate a mungrel church here, by imposing it upon them. But I do exceedingly admire when I read our history, to see how zealous and eager our nobility and people here were anciently to affert the right of our crown to the kingdom of France; whereas it is visible, that if we had kept France (for we conquered it intirely and fully) to this day, we must have run the fate of Arragon; and been, in time, ruined and opprest by our own valour and good fortune. A thing that was forefeen by the Macedonians, when their king Alexander had fubdued all Persia and the East; who weighing how probable it was, that their prince having the poffession of such great and flourishing kingdoms, should change his *domicilium imperii*; and inhabit in the centre of his dominions, and from

from thence govern Macedon; by which means the Grecians, who by their virtue and valour had conquered and subdued the barbarians, should in time (even as an effect of their victories) be opprest and tyrannized over by them: and this precautious foresight in the Greeks (as was fully believed in that age) hastened the fatal catastrophe of that great prince.

Doct. Well, I hope this consideration will fore-arm our parliaments, that they will not easily suffer their eyes to be dazzled any more with the false glory of conquering France.

Noble Ven. You need no great cautions against conquering France, at this present; and I believe your parliaments need as little admonition against giving of money towards new wars or alliances; that fine wheedle having lately lost them enough already: therefore, pray, let us suffer our friend to go on.

Eng. Gent. I have no more to say of foreign monarchies, but only to tell you; that Poland is both governed and possessed by some very great persons or potentates, called Palatines, and under them by a very

nume—

numerous gentry. For the king is not only elective, but so limited, that he has little or no power but to command their armies in time of war; which makes them often chuse foreigners of great fame for military exploits : and as for the commonalty or country-men, they are absolutely slaves, or villains. This government is extreamly confused ; by reason of the numerousness of the gentry : who do not always meet by way of representation as in other kingdoms ; but sometimes, for the choice of their king and upon other great occasions, collectively in the field ; as the tribes did at Rome : which would make things much more turbulent if all this body of gentry did not wholly depend for their estates upon the favour of the Palatines their lords, which makes them much more tractable. I have done with our neighbours beyond sea ; and should not without your command have made so long a digression in this place : which should indeed have been treated of before we come to speak of England, but that you were pleased to divert me from it before : However, being placed near the portraiture of our own country, it serves

better

better (as *comtraria juxta se posita*) to illuf-
trate it. But I will not make this deviation longer by apologizing for it ; and fhall
therefore defire you to take notice : that as
in England by degrees property came to
fhift from the few to the many, fo the government is grown heavier and more un-
eafy both to prince and people ; the complaints more in parliament ; the laws more
numerous, and much more tedious and pro-
lix : to meet with the tricks and malice of
men, which works in a loofe government :
for there was no need to make acts *verbofe,*
when the great perfons could prefently force
the execution of them. The law of Edward the firft for frequent parliaments, had
no more words than " a parliament fhall
" be holden every year ; " whereas our
act for a triennial parliament, in the time
of king Charles the firft, contained feveral
fheets of paper : to provide againft a failure
in the execution of that law. Which if
the power had remained in the lords, would
have been needlefs ; for fome of them, in
cafe of intermiffion of affembling the parliament, would have made their complaint
and addrefs to the king, and have immediately

diately removed the obstruction; which, in those days, had been the natural and easy way: but now that many of the lords, (like the bishops which the Popes make at Rome *in partibus infidelium*,) are meerly grown titular; and purchased for nothing but to get their wives place; it cannot be wondered at if the king slight their addresses, and the court-parasites deride their honourable undertakings for the safety of their country. Now the commons succeeding, as was said, in the property of the peers, and church; (whose lands, five parts of six, have been alienated; and mostly is come into the same hands, with those of the king and peers;) have inherited likewise, according to the course of nature, their power: but being kept from it by the established government, (which not being changed by any lawful acts of state, remains still in being formally, whereas virtually it is abolished) so that for want of outward orders and provisions, the people are kept from the exercise of that power, which is fallen to them by the law of nature: and those who cannot by that law pretend to the share they had, do yet enjoy it by virtue of

of that right which is now ceafed ; as having been but the natural effect of a caufe
that is no longer in being : and you know,
fublatâ causâ tollitur. I cannot fay that the
greater part of the people do know this
their condition, but they find very plainly
that they want fomething which they ought
to have ; and this makes them lay often the
blame of their unfettlednefs upon wrong
caufes : but however, are altogether unquiet
and reftlefs in the intervals of parliament ;
and when the king pleafes to affemble one,
fpend all their time in complaints of the
inexecution of the law ; of the multiplica-
tion of an infinity of grievances ; of mif-
fpending the publick monies ; of the danger
our religion is in by practifes to undermine
it and the ftate, by endeavours to bring in
arbitrary power ; and in queftioning great
officers of ftate, as the caufers and promo-
ters of all thefe abufes : in fo much, that
every parliament feems a perfect ftate of
war ; wherein the commons are tugging
and contending for their right, very juftly
and very honourably, yet without coming
to a point. So that the court fends them
packing ; and governs ftill worfe and worfe
in

in the vacancies, being neceſſitated thereunto by their deſpair of doing any good in
parliament ; and therefore are forced to uſe
horrid ſhifts to ſubſiſt without it, and to
keep it off : without ever conſidering, that
if theſe counſellors underſtood their trade,
they might bring the prince and people to
ſuch an agreement in parliament, as might
repair the broken and ſhipwrack'd government of England ; and in this ſecure the
peace, quiet and proſperity of the people,
the greatneſs and happineſs of the king, and
be themſelves not only out of preſent danger, (which no other courſe can exempt
them from,) but be renowned to all poſte-
rity.

Noble Ven. I beſeech you, ſir, how comes
it to paſs, that neither the king, nor any
of his counſellors could ever come to find
out the truth of what you diſcourſe ? for I
am fully convinced it is as you ſay.

Eng. Gent. I cannot reſolve you that ;
but this is certain, they have never endeavoured a cure, though poſſibly they
might know the diſeaſe : as fearing that
though the effects of a remedy would be,
as was ſaid, very advantagious both to king
and

and people, and to themfelves ; yet poffibly, fuch a reformation might not confift with the merchandize they make of the prince's favour ; nor with fuch bribes, gratuities and fees as they ufually take for the difpatch of all matters before them. And therefore our counfellors have been fo far from fuggefting any fuch thing to their mafter, that they have oppofed and quafhed all attempts of that kind : as they did the worthy propofals made by certain members of that parliament in the beginning of king James's reign, which is yet called the undertaking parliament. Thefe gentlemen confidering what we have been difcourfing of, *viz.* that our old government is at an end ; had framed certain heads, which, if they had been propofed by that parliament to the king, and by him confented to, would, in their opinion, have healed the breach : and that if the king would perform his part, that houfe of commons would undertake for the obedience of the people. They did believe that if this fhould have been moved in parliament before the king was acquainted with it, it would prove abortive ; and therefore fent three of their number to his majefty :

jefty : fir James Acroft, grandfather or father to the prefent bifhop of Hereford ; Thomas Harley, who was anceftor to the honourable family of that name in Herefordfhire ; and fir Henry Nevill, who had been ambaffador from queen Elizabeth to the French king. Thefe were to open the matter at large to the king, and to procure his leave that it might be propofed in parliament : which, after a very long audience and debate, that wife prince confented to ; with a promife of fecrefy in the mean time, which they humbly begged of his majefty. However, this took vent ; and the earl of Northampton, of the houfe of Howard, (who ruled the roft in that time) having knowledge of it, engaged fir R. Wefton, afterwards lord treafurer and earl of Portland, to impeach thefe undertakers in parliament, before they could move their matters : which he did the very fame day ; accompanying his charge, (which was endeavouring to alter the eftablifhed government of England) with fo eloquent an invective, that if one of them had not rifen, and made the houfe acquainted with the whole feries of the affair, they muft have been in danger

ger of being impeached by the commons;
but however it broke their defign, which
was all that Northampton and Wefton defired; and prevented pofterity from knowing any of the particulars of this reformation: for nothing being moved, nothing
could remain upon the journal. So that,
you fee, our predeceffors were not ignorant
altogether of our condition; though the
troubles which have befallen this poor kingdom fince, have made it much more appa-
rent; for fince the determination of that
parliament, there has not been one called,
(either in that king's reign, or his fon's, or
fince,) that hath not been diffolved abruptly; whilft the main bufineffes, and thofe
of moft concern to the publick, were depending and undecided. And although there
hath happened in this interim a bloody war,
which in the clofe of it, changed the whole
order and foundation of the polity of England; and that it hath pleafed God to reftore it again by his majefty's happy return,
fo that the old government is alive again:
yet it is very vifible that its deadly wound
is not healed; but that we are to this day
tugging with the fame difficulties, managing
the

the fame debates in parliament, and giving the fame difgufts to the court and hopes to the country, which our anceftors did before the year 1640 ; whilft the king hath been forced to apply the fame remedy of diffolution to his two firft parliaments, that his father ufed to his four firft and king James to his three laft, contrary to his own vifible intereft and that of his people : and this for want of having counfellors about him of abilities and integrity enough to difcover to him the difeafe of his government, and the remedy. Which I hope, when we meet to morrow morning you will come prepared to enquire into ; for the doctor fays, he will advife you to go take the air this afternoon in your coach.

Noble Ven. I fhall think it very long till the morning come : But before you go, pray give me leave to afk you fomething of your civil war here. I do not mean the hiftory of it, (although the world abroad is very much in the dark as to all your tranfactions of that time for want of a good one) but the grounds or pretences of it ; and how you fell into a war againft your king.

I   *Eng.*

Eng. Gen. As for our hiftory, it will not be forgotten. One of thofe who was in employment from the year 40 to 60, hath written the hiftory of thofe 20 years; a perfon of good learning and elocution : and though he be now dead, yet his executors are very unwilling to publifh it fo foon, and to rub a fore that is not yet healed. But the ftory is writ with great truth and impartiality ; although the author was engaged, both in councils and arms, for the parliament's fide. But for the reft of your demand, you may pleafe to underftand, that our parliament never did, as they pretended, make war againft the king : for he by law can do no wrong, and therefore cannot be quarrelled with. The war they declared was undertaken to refcue the king's perfon out of thofe mens hands who led him from his parliament, and made ufe of his name to levy a war againft them.

Noble Ven. But does your government permit, that in cafe of a difagreement between the king and his parliament, either of them may raife arms againft the other?

Eng. Gent. It is impoffible that any government can go farther than to provide
for

for its own safety and preservation whilst it is in being, and therefore it can never direct what shall be done when itself is at an end; there being this difference between our bodies natural and politick, that the first can make a testament to dispose of things after his death, but not the other. This is certain, that where-ever any two co-ordinate powers do differ, and there be no power on earth to reconcile them otherwise, nor any umpire; they will, *de facto*, fall together by the ears. What can be done in this case *de jure*, look into your own countryman Machiavel, and into Grotius; who in his book, *De jure Belli ac Pacis*, treated of such matters long before our wars. As for the ancient politicians, they must needs be silent in the point, as having no mixt governments amongst them; and as for me, I will not rest my self in so slippery a place. There are great disputes about it in the parliament's declarations before the war; and something considerable in the king's answer to them; which I shall specifie immediately, when I have satisfied you how our war begun: which was in this manner. The long parliament, having pro-

cured

cured from the king his royal assent for their sitting till they were disolved by act; and having paid and sent out the Scottish army, and disbanded our own; went on in their debates for the settling and mending our government. The king, being displeased with them for it; and with himself for putting it out of his power to dissolve them, now the business which they pretended for their perpetuation was quite finished; takes an unfortunate resolution to accuse five principal men of the commons house, and one of the peers, of high-treason: which he prosecuted in a new unheard-of way, by coming with armed men into the commons house of parliament, to demand their members. But nothing being done, by reason of the absence of the five; and tumults of discontented citizens flocking to White-Hall and Westminster; the king took that occasion to absent himself from his parliament. Which induced the commons house to send commissioners to Hampton-Court, to attend his majesty with " a " remonstrance of the state of the king- " dom; " and an humble request to return to his parliament, for the redressing those

those grievances which were specified in that remonstrance. But the king otherwise counselled, goes to Windsor; and thence Northwards, till he arrived at York: where he summons in the militia, that is, the trained bands of the county; and besides, all the gentry: of which there was a numerous appearance. The king addressed himself to the latter with complaints against a prevailing party in parliament, which intended to take the crown from his head: that he was come to them, his loving subjects, for protection: and, in short, desired them to assist him with monies to defend himself by arms. Some of these gentlemen petitioned his majesty to return to his parliament; the rest went about the debate of the king's demands: who, in the mean time, went to Hull, to secure the magazine there; but was denied entrance by a gentleman whom the house had sent down to prevent the seizing it: who was immediately declared a traytor, and the king fell to raising of forces. Which coming to the knowledge of the house, they made this vote; " That the king, seduced by evil " counsel, intended to levy war against

I 3 " his

" his parliament and people, to de-
" stroy the fundamental laws and liberties
" of England, and to introduce an arbi-
" trary government; &c. " This was the
first time they named the king, and the
last. For in all their other papers, and in
their declaration to arm for their defence,
(which did accompany this vote,) they name
nothing but malignant counsellors. The
king's answer to these votes and this declaration, is that which I mentioned : wherein
his majesty denies any intention of invading
the government; with high imprecations
upon himself and posterity, if it were otherwise; and owns, that they have right to
maintain their laws and government. This
is to be seen in the paper it self, now extant : and this gracious prince never pretended, (as some divines have done for him,)
that his power came from God, and that
his subjects could not dispute it, nor ought
he to give any account of his actions (though
he should enslave us all) to any but him.
So that our war did not begin upon a point
of right; but upon a matter of fact. For
without going to lawyers or casuists to be
resolved, those of the people who believed
that

that the king did intend to deſtroy our liberties, joyned with the parliament; and thoſe
who were of opinion that the prevailing party in parliament did intend to deſtroy the
king or dethrone him, aſſiſted vigorouſly
his majeſty with their lives and fortunes.
And the queſtion, you were pleaſed to aſk,
never came: for both parties pretended
and believed they were in the right; and
that they did fight for, and defend the
government. But I have wearied you
out. ——

Noble Ven. No ſure, ſir! But I am infinitely obliged to you for the great care you
have taken and ſtill have uſed to inſtruct
me; and beg the continuance of it for to
morrow morning.

Eng. Gent. I ſhall be ſure to wait upon
you at nine a clock: but I ſhall beſeech both
of you to bethink yourſelves what to offer;
for I ſhall come with a deſign to learn, not
to teach: nor will I preſume in ſuch a matter to talk all, as you have made me do to
day; for what I have yet to ſay in the point
of cure is ſo little, that it will look like
the mouſe to the mountain of this day's
diſcourſe.

Doct.

Doct. It is fo in all arts ; the corollary is fhort : and in ours, particularly. Thofe who write of the feveral difeafes incident to humane bodies, muft make long difcourfes of the caufes, fymptoms, figns and prognofticks of fuch diftempers ; but when they come to treat of the cure, it is difpatched in a few recipes.

Eng. Gent. Well, fir, for this bout, I humbly take my leave of you. ----- Nay, fir, you are not in a condition to ufe ceremony.

Doct. Sir, I forbid you this door ; pray retire. ---- To ftand here, is worfe than to be in the open air.

Noble Ven. I obey you both.

Doct. I fhall wait on you in the evening.

The

The THIRD DIALOGUE.

Noble Ven. GEntlemen, you are very welcome : what, you are come both together!

Doct. I met this gentleman at the door but methinks we fit looking one upon another, as if all of us were afraid to fpeak.

Eng. Gent. Do you think we have not reafon, in fuch a fubject as this is ? How can any man, without hefitation, prefume to be fo confident as to deliver his private opinion in a point, upon which for almoft two hundred year (for fo long our government has been crazy) no man has ventured ? and when parliaments have done any thing towards it, there have been animofities, and breaches, and at length civil wars ?

Noble Ven. Our work to day, is to endeavour to fhew, how all thefe troubles may be prevented for the future, by taking away the caufe of them ; which is the want of a good government : and therefore it will not be fo much prefumption in you, as charity, to declare yourfelf fully in this matter,

Eng. Gent. The cure will follow natu-rally

rally, if you are satisfied in the disease and in the cause of the disease. For if you agree that our government is broken; and that it is broken, because it was founded upon property, and that foundation is now shaken : it will be obvious, that you must either bring property back to your old government, and give the king and lords their lands again ; or else you must bring the government to the property, as it now stands.

Doct. I am very well satisfied in your grounds : but because this fundamental truth is little understood amongst our people; and that in all conversations men will be offering their opinions of what the parliament ought to do at their meeting ; it will not be amiss to examine some of those expedients they propose : and to see whether some, or all of them, may not be effectual towards the bringing us to some degree of settlement ; rather than to venture upon so great a change and alteration, as would be necessary to model our government anew.

Eng. Gent. Sir, I believe there can be no expedients proposed in parliament, that will not take up as much time and trouble ; find as much difficulty in passing with the

king

king and lords ; and feem as great a change
of government, as the true remedy would
appear : at leaft I fpeak as to what I have
to propofe. But however, I approve your
method : and if you will pleafe to propofe
any of thofe things, I fhall either willingly
embrace them ; or endeavour to fhew reafon, why they will be of little fruit in the
fettling our ftate.

Doƈt. I will reduce them to two heads,
(befides the making good laws for keeping
out arbitrary power, which is always underftood ;) the hindering the growth of popery, and confequently the providing againft
a popifh fucceffor ; and then declaring the
duke of Monmouth's right to the crown,
after it hath been examined and agreed to
in parliament.

Eng. Gent. As for the making new laws,
I hold it abfolutely needlefs ; thofe we have
already againft arbitrary power being abundantly fufficient, if they might be executed :
but that being impoffible (as I fhall fhew
hereafter) till fome change fhall be made,
I fhall poftpone this point. And for the
firft of your other two, I fhall divide and
feparate the confideration of the growth of

I 6

popery,

popery from that of the succession. I am
sorry that in the prosecution of this argument, I shall be forced to say something that
may not be very pleasing to this worthy
gentleman, we being necessiated to discourse
with prejudice of that religion which he pro-
fesses ; but it shall be with as little ill breed-
ing as I can, and altogether without passion
or invectives.

Noble Ven. It would be very hard for me
to suspect any thing from you that should be
disobliging : but pray, sir, go on to your political discourse. For I am not so ignorant myself but to know, that the conser-
vation of the national religion (be it what
it will) is essential to the well ordering a
state. And though in our city the doctri-
nals are very different from what are pro-
fessed here ; yet as to the government of the
state, I believe you know, that the pope or
his priests have as little influence upon it,
as your clergy have here, or in any part of
the world.

Eng. Gent. I avow it fully, sir ; and
with the favour you give, will proceed. It
cannot be denied but that, in former times,
popery has been very innocent here to the
government ; and that the clergy and the
pope

pope were so far from opposing our liberties, that they both sided with the barons to get a declaration of them by means of Magna Charta. It is true also that if we were all papists, and that our state were the same both as to property and empire as it was four hundred years ago, there would be but one inconvenience to have that religion national again in England : which is, that the clergy, *quatenus* such, had and will have a share in the soveraignty ; and inferiour courts in their own power, called ecclesiastical. This is, and ever will be, a solecifm in government ; besides a manifest contradiction to the words of Christ our Saviour, who tells us his kingdom is not of this world. And the truth is, if you look into the scriptures, you will find that the apostles did not reckon that the religion they planted should be national in any country ; and therefore have given no precepts to the magistrate to meddle in matters of faith and the worship of God : but preach'd, that Christians should yield them obedience in all lawfull things. There are many passages in holy writ which plainly declare, that the true believers and faints should be

but

but a handful, and such as God had separa-
ted, and as it were taken out of the world;
which would not have been said by them, if
they had believed that whole nations and
people should have been true followers of
Christ and of his flock: for certainly none
of them are to be damn'd; and yet Christ
himself tells us, that few are saved; and
bids us strive to get in at the strait gate.
And therefore I conceive it not to be imaginable, that either Christ or his apostles
did ever account, that the true religion
should be planted in the world by the framing of laws, catechisms, or creeds; by the
soveraign powers and magistrates, whether
you call them spiritual or temporal: but
that it should have a progress suitable to its
beginning. For it is visible that it had its
original from the power and spirit of God;
and came in against the stream: not only
without a Numa Pompilius, or a Mahomet,
to plant and establish it by humane constitutions and authority; but had all the laws
of the world to oppose it, and all the bloody
tyrants of that age to persecute it, and to
inflict exquisite torments on the professors of
it. In Nero's time (which was very early)
the

the Chriſtians were offered a temple in
Rome, and in what other cities they pleaſed,
to be built to Jeſus Chriſt ; and that the
Romans ſhould receive him into the number of their gods ; but our religion being
then in its purity, this was unanimouſly re-
fuſed ; for that ſuch a God muſt have no
companions, nor needed no temples ; but,
muſt be worſhiped in ſpirit and truth. The
ſucceſſors to theſe good Chriſtians were not
ſo ſcrupulous : for within ſome ages after,
the prieſts to get riches and power, and the
emperors to get and keep the empire, (for
by this time the Chriſtians were grown numerous and powerful,) combined together
to ſpoil our holy religion, to make it fit for
the government of this world ; and to introduce into it all the ceremonious follies and
ſuperſtitions of the heathen ; and (which is
worſe) the power of prieſts, both over the
perſons and conſciences of men. I ſhall ſay
no more of this ; but refer you to innumerable authors who have treated of this ſub-
ject : particularly to a French miniſter, who
hath written a book entituled, *La Religion
catholique apoſtolique Romaine inſtituee par
Nume Pompile* ; and to the incomparable
I   Machiavel

Machiavel in his poſthumous Letter, printed lately in our language with the tranſla-
tion of his works. But I have made a
long digreſſion : and to come back again,
ſhall only deſire you to take notice, when
I ſay that anciently popery was no inconvenience in this kingdom, I mean only
politically, as the government then ſtood ;
and do not ſpeak at all of the prejudice
which mens ſouls did and will ever receive
from the belief of thoſe impious tenents,
and the want of having the true goſpel of
Jeſus Chriſt preached unto them, living in
perpetual ſuperſtition and idolatry. But
the conſideration of theſe matters is not ſo
proper to my preſent purpoſe, being to diſcourſe only of government. Notwithſtand-
ing therefore, as I ſaid before, that popery
might have ſuited well enough with our
old conſtitution ; yet as to the preſent eſtate
which inclines to popularity, it would be
wholly as inconſiſtent with it, and with the
power of the keys and the empire of
prieſts, (eſpecially where there is a foreign
juriſdiction in the caſe,) as with the tyranny and arbitrary power of any prince in
the world. I will add thus much in confirmation

firmation of the Doctor's affertion, that
we ought to prevent the growth of popery,
fince it is now grown a dangerous faction
here againft the ftate.

Noble Ven. How can that be, I befeech
you, fir ?

Eng. Gent. Sir, I will make you judge
of it yourfelf. I will fay nothing of thofe
foolifh writings that have been put forth by
Mariana, Emanuel Sa, and fome others,
about the lawfulnefs of deftroying princes
and ftates in cafe of herefie : becaufe all
the confcientious and honeft papifts, (of
which I know there are great numbers in
the world,) do not only not hold, but even
abhor fuch curfed tenents ; and do believe,
that when the pope, by excommunication
hath cut off any prince from the commu-
nion of the church, he can go no further ;
nor ought to pretend a power to deprive
him of his crown, or abfolve his fubjects
from their oaths and obedience. But I fhall
confine my felf to the prefent condition of
our papifts here. You know how dangerous it is for any kingdom or ftate to have
a confiderable, wealthy, flourifhing party a-
mongft them, whofe intereft it is to deftroy
the

the polity and government of the country
where they live ; and therefore if our papists
prove this party, you will not wonder why
this people are fo eager to deprefs them.
This is our cafe : for in the beginning of
queen Elizabeth's reign, there was an alteration of religion in our country ; which
did fufficiently enrage the holy father at
Rome, to fee that this good cow would be
milked no longer.   He declares her an he-
retick and a baftard, (his fanctity not having
declared null that inceftuous marriage which
her father had contracted before with his
brother's wife, and which that king had diffolved to marry her mother) and afterwards
excommunicated our queen, depriving her,
as much as in him lay, of the kingdom.
Some of the zealots of that party, (having a
greater terrour for thofe thunder-bolts than
I believe many have now,) began to confpire againft her : and plots grew at length
fo frequent, and fo dangerous, that it was
neceffary (as the parliaments then thought)
to fecure the queen, by making fevere laws
againft a people, who did not believe themfelves her majefty's fubjects ; but on the
contrary, many of them thought themfelves
                                              in

in confcience obliged to oppofe and deftroy
her.   And although that excommunication,
as alfo the pretended doubtfulnefs of the
title, both died with that renowned queen;
yet a new defperate confpiracy againft the
king her fucceffor and the whole parliament enfuing not long after her deceafe,
thofe rigorous laws have been fo far from
being repealed, that very many more (and
far feverer) have been fince made, and are
yet in force. Now thefe laws make fo great
a diftinction between proteftants and
papifts, that whereas the former are by our
government and laws the freeft in the world,
the latter are little better than flaves; are
confined to fuch a diftance from their houfes; are not to come near the court; (which
being kept in the capital city, moftly deprives them from attending their neceffary
occafions) they are to pay two third parts
of their eftates annually to the king; their
priefts are to fuffer as traytors, and they as
felons for harbouring them.   In fine one of
us, if he do not break the municipal laws
for the good government of the country,
need not fear the king's power; whereas,
their being what they are is a breach of the
law;

law; and does put them into the prince's
hands to ruin them when he pleafes: nay,
he is bound by oath to do it; and when he
does it not, is complained againſt by his people, and parliaments take it amiſs. Now
judge you, ſir, whether it is not the intereſt
of theſe people to deſire and endeavour a
change, whilſt they remain under theſe diſ-
couragements; and whether they are not
like to join with the prince, (whoſe conni-
vance at the inexecution of thoſe laws is
the only means and hope of their prefervation,) whenever he ſhall undertake any
thing for the increaſe of his own power,
and the depreſſing his parliaments.

Noble Ven. What you ſay is very undeniable; but then the remedy is very eaſy
and obvious, as well as very juſt and honourable, which is the taking away thoſe
cruel laws; and if that were done they
would be one people with you; and would
have no neceſſity, and by conſequence no
deſire to engreaten the king againſt the intereſt and liberty of their own country.

Eng. Gent. You ſpeak very well; and
one of the reaſons amongſt many which I
have to deſire a compoſure of all our troubles

bles by a fettled government, is that I may
fee thefe people (who are very confiderable,
moft of them, for eftates, birth and breed-
ing) live quietly under our good laws ; and
increafe our trade and wealth with their expences here at home : whereas now the fe-
verity of our laws againft them, makes them
fpend their revenues abroad, and inrich o-
ther nations with the ftock of England.
But as long as the ftate here is fo unfettled
as it is, our parliaments will never confent
to countenance a party, who by the leaft
favour and indulgence may make themfelves
able to bring in their own religion to be national, and fo ruin our polity and liberties.

Noble Ven. I wonder why you fhould
think that poffible ?

Eng. Gent. Firft, fir, for the reafon we
firft gave, which is the crazinefs of our
polity : there being nothing more certain,
than that both in the natural and alfo the
politick body any finifter accident that in-
tervenes, during a very difeafed habit, may
bring a dangerous alteration to the patient.
An infurrection in a decayed government, a
thing otherwife very inconfiderable, has
proved very fatal ; as I knew a flight flefh-
wound

wound bring a lufty man to his grave in our wars, for, that he being extreamly infected with the French difeafe, could never procure the orifice to clofe. So although the defigns both at home and abroad for altering our religion, would be very little formidable to a well-founded government; yet in fuch an one as we have now, it will require all our care to obviate fuch machinations. Another reafon is the little zeal that is left amongft the ordinary proteftants: which zeal ufes to be a great inftrument of preferving the religion eftablifh'd; as it was here in queen Elizabeth's time. I will add, the little credit the church of England hath amongft the people; moft men being almoft as angry with that popery which is left amongft us (in furplices, copes, altars, cringings, bifhops, ecclefiaftical courts, and the whole hierarchy; befides an infinite number of ufelefs, idle, fuperftitious ceremonies; and the ignorance and vicioufnefs of the clergy in general) as they are with thofe dogma's that are abolifhed: fo that there is no hopes that popery can be kept out, but by a company of poor people called fanaticks, who are driven into corners

hers as the first Christians were; and who
only in truth conserve the purity of Christian religion, as it was planted by Christ and
his apostles and is contained in scripture.
And this makes almost all sober men believe,
that the national clergy, besides all their o-
ther good qualities, have this too; that
they cannot hope to make their hierarchy
subsist long against the scriptures, the hatred
of mankind, and the interest of this people,
but by introducing the Roman religion; and
getting a foreign head and supporter, which
shall from time to time brave and hector the
king and parliament in their favour and behalf: which yet would be of little advantage to them, if we had as firm and wise a
government as you have at Venice. Another reason, and the greatest, why the Ro-
mish religion ought to be very warily provided against at this time, is; that the lawful and undoubted heir to the crown, if
his majesty should die without legitimate
issue, is more than suspected to imbrace
that faith: which (if it should please God
to call the king, before there be any remedy applied to our distracted state) would
give a great opportunity by the power he
would

would have in intervals of parliament either to introduce immediately that profession, with the help of our clergy, and other English and foreign aids; or else to make so fair a way for it, that a little time would perfect the work. And this is the more formidable, for that he is held to be a very zealous and bigotted Romanist; and therefore may be supposed to act any thing to that end, although it should manifestly appear to be contrary to his own interest and quiet: so apt are those who give up their faith and the conduct of their lives to priests, (who to get to themselves empire, promise them the highest seats in heaven; if they will sacrifice their lives, fortunes, and hopes, for the exaltation of their holy mother, and preventing the damnation of an innumerable company of souls which are not yet born) to be led away with such erroneous and wild fancies. Whereas Philip the second of Spain, the house of Guise in France, and other great statesmen, have always made their own greatness their first aim; and used their zeal as an instrument of that: and, instead of being cozen'd by priests, have cheated them; and made them

endea-

endeavour to preach them up to the empire of the world. So I have done with the growth of popery ; and muſt conclude that, if that ſhould be ſtopt in ſuch manner that there could not be one papiſt left in England, and yet our polity left in the ſame diſorder that now afflicts it, we ſhould not be one ſcruple the better for it nor the more at quiet : the growth and danger of popery not being the cauſe of our preſent diſtemper, but the effect of it. But as a good and ſettled government would not be at all the nearer, for the deſtruction of popery ; ſo popery and all the dangers and inconveniences of it would not only be further off, but would wholly vaniſh, at the ſight of ſuch a reformation. And ſo we begin at the wrong end, when we begin with religion before we heal our breaches. I will borrow one ſimilitude more, with our doctor's favour, from his profeſſion. I knew once a man given over by the phyſicians, of an incurable Cachexia ; which they ſaid proceeded from the ill quality of the whole maſs of blood, from great aduſtion, and from an ill habit of the whole body : the patient had very often painful fits of the

K   colick

colick, which they faid proceeded from
the fharpnefs of the humour which caufed
the difeafe ; and, amongft the reft, had one
fit which tormented him to that degree,
that it was not expected he could out-live
it ; yet the doctors delivered him from it in
a fmall time : notwithftanding, foon after
the man died of his firft diftemper. Whereas, if their art had arrived to have cured
that which was the caufe of the other, the
colick had vanifh'd of itfelf and the patient recovered. I need make no application :
nor fhall need to fay much of the fucceffion
of the crown, (which is my next province,)
but this I have faid already ; that it is needlefs to make any provifion againft a popifh
fucceffor, if you rectifie your government ;
and if you do not, all the care and
circumfpection you can ufe in that particular will be ufelefs and of none effect ;
and will but at laft (if it do not go off eafily,
and the next heir fucceed peaceably, as is
moft likely, efpecially if the king live till
the people's zeal and mettle is over) end
probably in a civil war about title : and then
the perfon deprived may come in with his
fword in his hand, and bring in upon the
point of it both the popifh religion, and arbitrary

bitrary power. Which, though I believe he will not be able to maintain long, (for the reasons before alledged,) yet that may make this generation miserable and unhappy. It will certainly be agreed by all lovers of their country, that popery must be kept from returning and being national in this kingdom ; as well for what concerns the honour and service of God, as the welfare and liberty of the people. And I conceive there are two ways, by which the parliament may endeavour to secure us against that danger. The first, by ordering such a change in the administration of our government, that whoever is prince can never violate the laws ; and then we may be very safe against popery, (our present laws being effectual enough to keep it out, and no new ones being like to be made in parliament that may introduce it ;) and this remedy will be at the same time advantagious to us, against the tyranny and incroachments of a protestant successor ; so that we may call it an infallible remedy both against popery and arbitrary power. The second way is, by making a law to disable any papists (by name, or otherwise) from inheriting the

crown ;

crown ; and this is certainly fallible, that is, may possibly not take place (as I shall shew immediately :) and besides it is not improbable that an heir to this kingdom in future times, may diffemble his religion till he be seated in the throne ; or possibly be perverted to the Roman faith after he is possest of it, when it may be too late to limit his prerogative in parliament : and to oppose him without that will, I fear, be judged treason.

Doct. But sir, would you have the parliament do nothing, as things stand, to provide (at least as much as in them lies) that whoever succeeds be a good protestant ?

Eng. Gent. Yes, I think it best in the first place to offer to his majesty the true remedy ; and if they find him averse to that, then to pursue the other which concerns the succession : because the people (who are their principals and give them their power) do expect something extraordinary from them at this time ; and the most of them believe this last the only present means to save them from popery, which they judge (and very justy) will bring in with it a change of government.

But

But then, I suppose, they may be encouraged to propose, in the first place, the true cure : not only because that is infallible, as has been proved ; but likewise because his majesty in probability will sooner consent to any reasonable demand towards the reforming of the government and to the securing us that way, than to concur to the depriving his only brother of the crown. And possibly this (as I said before) may be the only way the parliament can hope will prove effectual : for if you please to look but an age back into our story, you will find that Henry the eighth did procure an act of parliament, which gave him power to dispose of the crown by his last will and testament ; and that he did accordingly make his said will, and by it devise the succession to his son Edward the sixth, in the first place, and to the heirs of his body ; and for want of such, to his daughter Mary, and to the heirs of her body ; and for want of which heirs, to his daughter Elizabeth (our once soveraign, of immortal and blessed memory) and the heirs of her body ; and for want of all such issue, to the right heirs of his younger sister ; who was,

K 3

be-

before he made this will, married to Charles
Brandon duke of Suffolk, and had issue by
him. By this testament he disinherited his
elder sister; who was married in Scotland:
and by that means did, as much as in him
lay, exclude his majesty (who now, by
God's mercy, reigns over us) as also his
father and grandfather. And to make the
case stronger, there passed an act long after, in the reign of queen Elizabeth; that
it should be treason during that queen's
life, and a premunire afterwards, to assert
that the imperial crown of England could
not be disposed of by act of parliament.
Yet after the decease of that queen, there
was no considerable opposition made to the
peaceable reception and recognition of king
James of happy memory: and those who
did make a little stir about the other title,
as the lord Cobham, sir Walter Rawleigh,
and a few others, were apprehended and
condemn'd according to law. And notwithstanding that, since, in the reign of
king Charles the first, there was a bloody
civil war, in which men's minds were ex-
asperated at a high rate, yet in all the course
of it the original want of title was never
objected

objected againſt his late majeſty. I do not
urge this to aver that the parliament with
the king's conſent cannot do lawfully this,
or any other great matter ; (which would
be an incurring the penalty of that law, and
a ſoleciſm in the politicks :) but to ſhew,
that when the paſſions of men are quieted,
and the reaſons other than they were, it happens oftentimes that thoſe acts which concern the ſucceſſion fall to the ground of
themſelves ; and that even without the
ſword, which in this caſe was never adoperated : and that therefore this remedy in
our caſe may be likely never to take place,
if it pleaſe God the king live till this nation
be under other kind of circumſtances.

Doct. Sir, you ſay very well : but it ſeems
to me, that the laſt parliament was in ſome
kind of fault, if this be true that you ſay :
for I remember that my lord chancellor did
once during their ſitting, in his majeſty's
name, offer them to ſecure their religion
and liberties any way they could adviſe of,
ſo they would let alone meddling with the
ſucceſſion ; and invited them to make
any propoſals they thought neceſſary to
that end.

Eng. Gent. Hinc illæ lacrymæ ! If this had been all, we might have been happy at this time : but this gracious offer was, *in limine,* accompanied with such conditions that made the parliament conjecture that it was only to perplex and divide them ; and did look upon it as an invention of some new Romanza, (counsellers and those too, possibly, influenced by the French) to make them embrace the shadow for the substance ; and satisfying themselves with this appearance, to do their ordinary work of giving money, and be gone and leave the business of the kingdom as they found it. For it was proposed, that whatsoever security we were to receive should be both conditional, and reversionable. That is, first, we should not be put into possession of this new charter (be it what it will) till after the death of his majesty who now is : whereas such a provision is desirable, and indeed necessary for us for this only reason ; that when that unfortunate hour comes, we might not be (in that confusion) unprovided of a calm, settled and orderly, as well as a legal way, to keep out popery : whereas otherwise if we be to take possession in that minute, it must

muft either mifcarry, or be gotten by a
war. If it be true that poffeffion be nine
points of the law, in other cafes, it is in
this the whole ten : and I fhould be very
unwilling in fuch a diftraction to have no
fanctuary to fly to, but a piece of parchment kept in the pells ; and to have this
too, as well as other advantages, in the
power and poffeffion of him in whofe prejudice it was made. This had been almoft
as good an expedient to keep out popery, as
the bill which was thrown out that parliament ; which provided, that in the reign
of a king, that fhould be a papift, the bifhops fhould chufe one another upon vacancies. Thofe counfellors who put my lord
chancellor upon this propofal, were either
very flender politicians themfelves ; or elfe
thought the parliament fo. If *Magna
Charta*, and the petition of right, had not
been to take place till after the deceafe of
thofe princes who confirmed them, neither
had the barons fhed their blood to fo good
purpofe ; nor the members of the parliament in *tertio Caroli*, deferved fo glorious
an imprifonment, after it was ended. The
other condition, in this renowned propofal,

K 5

is ;

is ; that all provision and security which is
given us to preserve our religion shall cease
immediately, whenever the prince shall take
a certain oath to be penned for that purpose : and I leave it to all thinking men to
determine what that will avail us, when
we shall have a king of that profession over
us, who shall not have so much zeal for his
religion, as he who is now the next successor
hath ; but shall possibly prefer his ambition,
and his desire to get out of wardship, before the scruples of his confessor ; and yet
may afterwards, by getting absolution for,
and dispensation from such oaths and com-
pliance, imploy the power he gets himself,
and the security he deprives us of, to introduce violently what worship and faith he
pleases. This gracious offer had the fatality
to disgust one of the best parliaments that
ever sate, and the most loyal : so that laying it aside, they fell upon the succession
(the only thing they had then left) and were
soon after dissolved : leaving the kingdom
in a more distracted condition than they
found it. And this can no way be compo-
sed, but by mending the polity ; so that
whoever is king cannot (be he never so inclined

clined to it) introduce popery, or deftroy whatever religion fhall be eftablifhed. As you fee in the example of the dutchy of Hanover: whofe prince, fome fourteen years fince, was perverted to the Roman church; went to Rome to abjure herefie, (as they call the truth;) return'd home; where he lived and governed as he did before; without the leaft animofity of his fubjects for his change, or any endeavour of his to introduce any in his government or people: and dying this laft fpring, left the peaceable and undifturbed rule of his fubjects to the next fucceffor, his brother the bifhop of Ofnaburg, who is a proteftant. And this becaufe the polity of that dukedom has been conferved entire for many years, and is upon a right bafis: and if our cafe were fo, we fhould not only be out of danger to have our religion altered (as I faid before) whoever is king, but fhould in other things be in a happy and flourifhing condition. But I have made a long and tedious digreffion to anfwer your demands: now 'tis time you affift me to find the natural cure of all our mifchiefs.

K 6

Doct.

Doct. Stay, fir; I confefs myfelf to be wonderfully edified with your difcourfe hitherto, but you have faid nothing yet of the duke of Monmouth.

Eng. Gent. I do not think you defire it, though you were pleafed to mention fuch a thing; for I fuppofe you cannot think it poffible, that this parliament (which is now fpeedily to meet by his majefty's gracious proclamation) can ever fuffer fuch a thing to be fo much as debated amongft them.

Doct. Sir, you have no reafon to take that for granted, when you fee what books are printed; what great and honourable perfons frequent him in private, and countenance him in publick; what fhoals of the middle fort of people have in his progrefs this fummer met him before he came into any great town; and what acclamations and bon-fires have been made in places where he lodged.

Eng. Gent. Thefe things, I muft confefs, fhew how great a diftemper the people are in; and the great reafon we have to pray God of his mercy to put an end to it by a happy agreement in parliament. But certainly this proceeds only from the hatred

3   they

they have to the next fucceffor and his religion; and from the compaffion they have to
the duke of Monmouth (who as they fuppofe, hath fuffered banifhment and dif-
favour at court, at his inftance;) and not
from any hopes, or expectations, that the
parliament will countenance any pretence
that can be made in his behalf to the fucceffion.

Doct. It may be when we have difcourfed of it, I fhall be of your mind; as indeed I am inclined already. But yet as nothing in war is more dangerous than to con-
temn an enemy; fo in this argumentation
that we ufe to fecure our liberties, we muft
leave nothing unanfwered that may ftand
in the way of that; especially the duke of
Monmouth's claim, which is pretended to
confirm and fortifie them: for (fay fome
men) if you fet him up, he will prefently
pafs all bills that fhall concern the fafety
and intereft of the people; and fo we fhall
be at reft forever.

Eng. Gent. Well, I fee I muft be more
tedious than I intended. Firft then, the
reafoning of thefe men you fpeak of, does
in my apprehenfion fuppofe a thing, I cannot

not mention without horrour; which is, that this person should be admitted immediately to the possession of the crown, to do all these fine matters. For otherwise, if he must stay till the death of our soveraign who now reigns, (which I hope and pray will be many years,) possibly these delicate bills may never pass; nor he find hereafter the people in so good a humour to admit him to the reversion; which if it could be obtain'd (as I think it impossible politically) yet the possession must be kept by a standing army; and the next successor cannot have a better game to play, nor a better adversary to deal with, than one who leaps in over the heads of almost all the protestant princes families abroad; (besides some papists who are greater:) and when we have been harrassed with wars and the miseries that accompany it some few years, you shall have all these fine people, who now run after him, very weary of their new prince. I would not say any thing to disparage a person so highly born, and of so early merit; but this I may say, that if a lawful title should be set on foot in his favour, and a thousand Dutch hosts and such like should

swear

fwear a marriage, yet no fober man that is not blinded with prejudice will believe, that our king (whom none can deny to have an excellent underftanding) would ever marry a woman fo much his inferiour as this great perfon's mother was; and this at a time when his affairs were very low, and he had no vifible or rational hopes to be reftored to the poffeffion of his kingdoms, but by an affiftance which might have been afforded him by means of fome great foreign alliance. Well, but to leave all this, do thefe men pretend that the duke of Monmouth fhall be declared fucceffor to the crown in parliament, with the king's concurrence, or without it? If without it, you muft make a war for it; and I am fure that no caufe can be ftated upon fuch a point, that will not make the afferters and undertakers of it be condemned by all the politicians and moralifts of the world, and by the cafuifts of all religions: and fo by confequence, it is like to be a very unfuccefsful War. If you would have this declar'd with the king's confent; either you fuppofe the royal affent to be given, when the king has his liberty either to grant it or not

not grant it, to diffolve the parliament or not diffolve it, without ruin or prejudice to his affairs : if in the firft cafe, it is plain he will not grant it, becaufe he cannot do it without confeffing his marriage to that duke's mother, which he hath already declared againft in a very folemn manner, and caufed it to be regiftred in chancery ; and which not only no good fubject can chufe but believe, but which cannot be doubted by any rational perfon: for it would be a very unnatural, and indeed a thing unheard of, that a father who had a fon in lawful matrimony, and who was grown to perfection, and had fignalized himfelf in the wars, and who was ever intirely beloved by him, fhould difinherit him by fo folemn an affeveration (which muft be a falfe one too) to caufe his brother to fucceed in his room. And whereas it is pretended by fome, that his majefty's danger from his brother's counfels and defigns may draw from him fomething of this : befide that they do not much complement the king in this ; it is clear, his brother is not fo popular; but that he may fecure him when he pleafes without hazard, if there were any ground for fuch

an

an apprehenfion. But we muft in the next place fuppofe that the king's affairs were in fuch a pofture, that he could deny the parliament nothing without very great mifchief and inconvenience to himfelf and the kingdom: then I fay, I doubt not, but the wifdom of the parliament will find out divers demands and requefts to make to his majefty of greater benefit, and more necef-fary for the good of his people than this would be; which draws after it not only a prefent unfettlednefs, but the probable ha-zard of mifery and devaftation for many years to come, as has been proved. So that as on the one fide, the parliament could not make a more unjuftifiable war than up-on this account; fo they could not be dif-folved upon any occafion wherein the peo-ple would (not fhew lefs difcontent and re-fentment, and for which the courtiers would not hope to have a better pretext to ftrive in the next choice to make their arts and endeavours more fuccefsful in the election of members more fuitable to their defigns for the continuance of this prefent mif-government: for if this parliament do mif-fpend the peoples mettle which is now up,

in

in driving that nail which cannot go; they
muft look to have it cool, and fo the fhip
of this commonwealth, which if they pleafe
may be now in a fair way of entering into
a fafe harbour, will be driven to fea again
in a ftorm; and muft hope for, and expect
another favourable wind to fave them: and
God knows when that may come.

Doct. But, fir, there are others, who
not minding whether the parliament will
confider the duke of Monmouth's concern
fo far as to debate it, do yet pretend that
there is great reafon to keep up the peoples
affections to him; and poffibly to foment
the opinion they have of his title to the
crown: to the end, that if the king fhould
die *re infecta,* (that is, before fuch time as
the government is redreft, or the duke of
York difabled by law to fucceed,) the people might have a head; under whofe command and conduct they might ftand upon
their guard, till they had fome way fecured
their government and religion.

Eng. Gent. What you have ftarted is not
a thing that can fafely be difcourfed of,
nor is it much material to our defign; which
is intended to fpeculate upon our government,

ment, and to fhew how it is decayed. I
have induftrioufly avoided the argument of
rebellion, as I find it coucht in modern politicians ; becaufe moft princes hold, that
all civil wars in mixt monarchies muft be
fo ; and a politician, (as well as an orator)
ought to be *vir bonus*; fo ought to difcourfe
nothing, how rational foever, in thefe points
under a peaceable monarchy which gives
him protection, but what he would fpeak
of his prince if all his counfel were prefent.
I will tell you only that thefe authors hold,
that nothing can be alledged to excufe the
taking arms by any people in oppofition
to their prince from being *crimen læfæ ma-
jeftatis*, but a claim to a lawful jurifdiction
or co-ordination in the government, by
which they may judge of and defend their
own rights ; and fo pretend to fight for and
defend the government. For though all do
acknowledge, that *populi falus* is, and ought
to be, the moft fupreme or foveraign law
in the world ; yet if we fhould make private perfons, how numerous foever, judge
of *populi falus*, we fhould have all the ri-
fings and rebellions that fhould ever be
made, juftified by that title : as happened in
France,

France, when *La Guerre du bien publique* took that name; which was raised by the insatiable ambition of a few noblemen, and by correspondency and confederacy with Charles, son of the duke of Burgundy, and other enemies to that crown.

Doct. But would you have our people do nothing then, if the king should be assassinated, or die of a natural death?

Eng. Gent. You ask me a very fine question, doctor. If I say, I would have the people stir in that case, then the king and his laws take hold of me; and if I should answer, that I would have them be quiet, the people would tear me in pieces for a Jesuit; or at least, believe that I had no sense of the religion, laws, and liberty of my country. *De facto,* I do suppose, that if the people do continue long in this heat which now possesseth them; and remain in such a passion at the time of the king's death without settling matters; they may probably fall into tumults and civil war: which makes it infinitely to be desired, and prayed for by all good Englishmen, that during the quiet and peace we enjoy by the blessing of his majesty's life and happy reign, we

we might likewife be fo wife and fortunate
as to provide for the fafety and profperity
of the next generation.

Doct. But if you would not have the
people in fuch a cafe take the duke of Monmouth for their head, what would you have
them do?

Eng. Gent. Doctor, you afk me very fine
queftions! Do not you know that Machiavel, the beft and moft honeft of all the
modern politicians, has fuffered fufficiently
by means of priefts, and other ignorant
perfons? who do not underftand his writings, and therefore impute to him the
teaching fubjects how they fhould rebel
and confpire againft their princes; which
if he were in any kind guilty of, he would
deferve all the reproaches that have been
caft upon him, and ten times more : and fo
fhould I, if I ventured to obey you in this.
I am very confident, that if any man
fhould come to you, to implore your fkill
in helping him to a drug that might quick-
ly, and with the leaft fear of being fufpect-
ed, difpatch an enemy of his, or fome
other, by whofe death he was to be a gain-
er; or fome-young lafs that had gotten a;
fur-

surreptitious great belly, should come to you to teach her how to destroy the fruit; I say, in this case you would scarce have had patience to hear these perfons out : much less would you have been so wicked to have in the least assisted them in their designs. No more than Solon, Lycurgus, Periander, or any other of the sages could have been brought to have given their advice to any persons who should have begged it, to enable them to ruin and undermine the government of their own commonwealths.

Doct. Sir, this reprehension would be very justly given me, if I had intended by this question to induce you to counsel me, or any other how to rebel. My meaning was to desire you (who have heretofore been very fortunate in prophesying concerning the events of our changes here) to exercise your faculty a little at this time; and tell us, what is like to be the end of these distractions we are under, in case we shall not be so happy as to put a period to them by mending our government and securing our religion and liberty in a regular way.

Eng. Gent. Doctor, I will keep the reputation of prophecy, which I have gained
with

with you; and not hazard it with any new
predictions, for fear they fhould mifcarry.
Yet I care not, if I gratify your curiofity
a little in the point about which you firft
began to interrogate me, by prefaging to
you ; that in cafe we fhould have troubles
and combuftions here, after his majefty's
deceafe, (which God avert) we muft expect a very unfuccefsful end of them, if we
fhould be fo rafh and unadvifed as to make
the great perfon we have been lately fpeaking of, our head ; and that nothing can be
more dangerous and pernicious to us than fuch
a choice. I have not in this difcourfe the leaft
intention to except againft, much lefs to difparage the perfonal worth of the duke of
Monmouth, which the world knows to be
very great ; but do believe that he hath
courage and conduct proportionable to any
imployment that can be conferred upon
him, whether it be to manage arms or
counfels : but my opinion is, that no perfon in his circumftance can be a proper head
in this cafe. For the people having been
already put on upon the fcent of his title to
the crown, will be very hardly called off;
and fo will force the wifer men, who may
defign

design better things, to consent that he be proclaimed king immediately : except there be some other head, who by his power, wisdom, and authority, may restrain the forwardness of the multitude; and obviate the acts of some men, whose interest and hopes may prompt them to foment the humours of the people. Now the consequences of hurrying a man to the throne so tumultuously, without the least deliberation, are very dismal : and do not only not cure the politick distemper of our country which we have talked so much of, but do infinitely augment it ; and add to the disease our state labours under already (which is a consumption) a very violent feaver too ; I mean war at home, and from abroad, which must necessarily follow in a few years : nor is it possible to go back, when once we have made that step ; for our new king will call a parliament, which being summoned by his writ, neither will nor can question his title or government, otherwise than by making addresses and by presenting bills to him, as they do to his now majesty.

Noble

Noble Ven. It feems to me, that there needs nothing more than that : for if he confent to all laws as fhall be prefented to him ; you may reform your government fufficiently, or elfe it is your own fault.

Eng. Gent. We have fhewed already, and fhall do more hereafter, that no laws can be executed till our government be mended : and if you mean we fhould make fuch as fhould mend that, (befides that it would be a better method to capitulate that, before you make choice of your prince, as wife people have done in all ages, and the cardinals do at Rome in the conclave before they choofe their Pope) I fay befides this, it is not to be taken for granted that any bills that tend to make confiderable alterations in the adminiftration, (and fuch we have need of as you will fee anon) would either in that cafe be offered, or confented to. Both prince and people being fo ready to cry out upon forty-one, and to be frighted with the name of a commonwealth; even now when we think popery is at the door : which fome people then will think farther off, and fo not care to make fo great alterations to keep it out. Befides, the

L

great men, and favourites of the new prince, will think it hard that the king should be so bounded and limited both in power and revenue, that he shall have no means to exercise his liberality towards them ; and so may use their interest and eloquence, in both houses, to dissuade them from pressing so hard upon a prince, who is a true zealous protestant, and has always headed that party ; and who is justly admired, if not adored by the people : and considering too, that all the power they leave him, will serve but to enable him to defend us the better from popery and arbitrary power; to prevent the latter of which most monarchies were originally instituted. Thus we may exercise, during a parliament or two, lovetricks between the prince and his people ; and imitate the hony-moon that continued for about two years after his majesty's restauration : till the ill management of affairs, and the new grievances that shall arise, (which will be sure never to fail till our true cure be effected, notwithstanding the care of the new king and his counsellers) shall awaken the discontents of the people : and then they will curse the time, in which they

they made this election of a prince; and the great men, for not hindering them. Then men will be reckoning up the discontents of the peers, sometime after they had made a rash choice of H. the 7th in the field, (who had then no title,) when they saw how he made use of the power they gave him; to leſſen their greatneſs and to fortifie himſelf, upon their ruins. When it comes to this, and that the governing party comes to be but a little faction; the people, who never know the true cauſe of their diſtemper, will be looking out abroad who has the lawful title; (if the next heir be not in the mean time with an army of Engliſh and ſtrangers in the field here, as is moſt likely:) and look upon the prince of Orange, or the next of kin, as their future ſaviour; in caſe the duke be dead in the mean time, and ſo the cauſe of all their diſtruſt taken away. Thus moſt men, (not only diſcontented perſons, but the people in general,) lookt upon his majeſty that now is, as their future deliverer, during our late diſtractions; when his condition was ſo weak that he had ſcarce wherewithall to ſubſiſt, and his enemies powerful

at home and victorious abroad : which will
not be, I fear, our cafe. I prophefy then,
(becaufe you will have me ufe this word,)
that if nobles or people make any fuch unfortunate choice as this, during the diftractions we may be in upon his majefty's death,
we fhall not only mifs our cure ; or have
it deferred, till another government make
it ; but remain in the confufion we now
fuffer under ; and befides that, fhall be fure
to feel, firft or laft, the calamity of a civil
and foreign war : and in the mean time to
be in perpetual fear of it, and fuffer all the
burden and charge which is neceffary to provide for it ; befides all the other ill confequences of a ftanding army. To conclude,
I affure you on the faith of a Chriftian,
that I have made this difcourfe folely and
fingly out of zeal and affection to the intereft of my country ; and not at all with
the leaft intention to favour or promote the
caufe or intereft of the duke of York, or
to difparage the duke of Monmouth : from
whom I never received the leaft unkindnefs ;
nor ever had the honour to be in his company : and to whom I fhall ever pay
refpect fuitable to his high birth and merit.

Noble

Noble Ven. Well, fir, your reafoning in this point has extreamly fatisfied me; and the doctor, I fuppofe, was fo before, as he averred; therefore pray let us go on where we left.

Eng. Gent. I cannot take fo much upon me as to be dictator in the method of our cure, fince either of you is a thoufand times better qualified for fuch an office; and therefore fhall henceforth defire to be an auditor.

Doct. pray, fir, let us not fpend time in compliments, but be pleafed to proceed in this bufinefs; and we doubt not but as you have hitherto wonderfully delighted us, fo you will gratifie us in concluding it.

Eng. Gent. I fee I muft obey you: but pray help me, and tell me in the firft place, whether you do not both believe, that as the *caufa caufarum* of all our diftractions is (as has been proved) the breach of our government, fo that the immediate caufes are two; firft, the great diftruft on both fides between the king, and his people and parliament; the firft fearing that his power will be fo leffened by degrees, that at length it will not be able to keep the crown upon his head: and the latter feeing all things in

L 3   diforder,

diforder, and that the laws are not executed, (which is the fecond of the two caufes,) fear the king intends to change the government and be arbitrary.

Noble Ven. I am a ftranger; but (though I never reflected fo much upon the original caufe, as I have done fince I heard you difcourfe of it) yet I ever thought, that thofe two were the caufes of the unquietnefs of this kingdom. I mean the jealoufy between the king and his people ; and the inexecution of the great law of calling parliaments annually, and letting them fit to difpatch their affairs : I underftand this in the time of his majefty's grand-father and father, more than in his own reign.

Eng. Gent. Then whoever can abfolutely lay thefe two caufes afleep for ever, will arrive to a perfect cure : which I conceive no way of doing, but that the king have a great deal more power, or a great deal lefs. And you know that what goes out of the king muft go into the people, and fo *vice verfa* ; infomuch that the people muft have a great deal more power, or a great deal lefs. Now it is no queftion, but either of thefe two would rather increafe their power,

than

than diminifh it: fo that if this cannot be
made up by the wifdom of this age, we
may fee in the next; that both the king
will endeavour to be altogether without a
parliament, and the parliament to be without a king.

Doct. I begin to fmell what you would
be nibbling at; the pretence which fome
had before his majefty's reftauration, of a
Commonwealth, or Democracy.

Eng. Gent. No; I abhor the thoughts of
wifhing, much lefs endeavouring, any fuch
thing, during the circumftances we are
now in: that is, under oaths of obedience
to a lawful king. And truly, if any Themiftocles fhould make to me fuch a propofal, I fhould give the fame judgment concerning it that Ariftides did in fuch a cafe.
The ftory is fhort. After the war between
the Greeks and the Perfians was ended,
and Xerxes driven out of Greece; the
whole fleet of the Grecian confederates,
(except that of Athens, which was gone
home) lay in a great arfenal (fuch as were
then in ufe) upon the coaft of Attica:
during their abode there. Themiftocles har-
rangues one day the people of Athens, (as

L 4

was then the custom,) and tells them, that he had a design in his head, which would be of infinite profit and advantage to the commonwealth : but that it could not be executed without the order and authority of them ; and that it did likewise require secrefy, and if it were declared there in the market-place, (where strangers as well as citizens might be present,) it could not be concealed ; and therefore proposed it to their consideration what should be done in it. It was at length concluded, that Themistocles should propose it to Aristides ; and if he did next morning acquaint the people that he gave his approbation to it, it should be proceeded in. Themistocles informs him, that the whole fleet of their confederates in the war against the Medes had betaken themselves to the great arsenal upon their coast, where they might be easily fired ; and then the Athenians would remain absolute masters of the sea, and so give law to all Greece. When Aristides came the next day to deliver his judgment to the people, he told them that the business proposed by Themistocles, was indeed very advantageous and profitable to the Athenians ;

ans; but withal, the moſt wicked and villainous attempt that ever was undertaken: upon which it was wholly laid aſide. And the ſame judgment do I give, doctor, of your Democracy, at this time. But to return to the place where I was; I do believe that this difference may eaſily be terminated very fairly; and that our houſe need not be pulled down, and a new one built; but may be very eaſily repair'd, ſo that it may laſt many hundred years.

Noble Ven. I begin to perceive that you aim at this; that the king muſt give the people more power, as Henry the third, and king John did; or the parliament muſt give the king more, as you ſaid they did in France in the time of Lewis the eleventh; or elſe that it will come in time to a war again.

Eng. Gent. You may pleaſe to know; that in all times hitherto, the parliament never demanded any thing of the king, wherein the intereſt and government of the kingdom was concerned, (excepting acts of pardon,) but they founded their demands upon their right; not only becauſe it might ſeem unreaſonable for them to be earneſt

with

with him, to give them that which was his own ; but also because they cannot chuse but know that all powers which are funda-mentally and lawfully in the crown, were placed there upon the first institution of our government, to capacitate the prince to govern and protect his people : so that for the parliament to seek to take from him such authority, were to be *felo de se,* as we call a self-homicide. But as in some distem-pers of the body the head suffers as well as the inferior parts, so that it is not possible for it to order, direct and provide for the whole body, as its office requires ; since the wisdom and power which is placed there, is given by God to that end : in which case, though the distemper of the body may be-gin from the disease of some other part, or from the mass of blood, or putrefaction of other humours ; yet since that noble part is so affected by it that reason and discourse fails, therefore to restore this again reme-dies must be apply'd to, and possibly hu-mours or vapours drawn from the head it-self ; that so it may be able to govern and reign over the body, as it did before : or else the whole man, like a slave, must be

ruled

ruled and guided *ab extrinfeco*, that is, by fome keeper: fo it is now with us, in our politick difeafe: where granting (if you pleafe) that the diftemper does not proceed from the head, but the corruption of other parts; yet in the cure, applications muft be made to the head as well as to the members, if we mean poor England fhall recover its former perfect health: and therefore it will be found, perhaps, effential to our being, to afk fomething (in the condition we now are) to which the king as yet may have a right; and which except he pleafe to part with, the phenomena of government cannot be falved; that is, our laws cannot be executed; nor *Magna Charta* itfelf made practicable: and fo both prince and people, that is the polity of England, muft die of this difeafe; or in this delirium, muft be governed *ab extrinfeco*; and fall to the lot of fome foreign power.

Noble Ven. But, fir, (fince the bufinefs is come to this dilemma) why may not the king afk more power of the parliament, as well as they of him?

Eng. Gent. No queftion but our prefent counfellors and courtiers would be nibbling

at

at that bait again, if they had another parliament that would take pensions for their votes; but in one that is come fresh from the people, and understand their sense and grievances very well, I hardly believe they will attempt it: for both council and parliament must needs know by this time-a-day, that the cause of all our distractions coming (as has been said an hundred times) from the king's having a greater power already, than the condition of property at this present can admit without confusion and disorder, it is not like to mend matters for them to give him more; except they will deliver up to him at the same instant their possessions and right to their lands, and become naturally and politically his slaves.

Noble Ven. Since there must be a voluntary parting with power, I fear your cure will prove long and ineffectual: and we reconcilers, shall, (I fear,) prove like our devout Capuchin at Venice. This poor man's name was Fra. Barnardino da Udine; and was esteemed a very holy man, as well as an excellent preacher: insomuch that he was appointed to preach the Lent sermons in one of our principal churches; which he

per-

performed at the beginning with so much eloquence, and applause, that the church was daily crouded three hours before the sermon was to begin. The esteem and veneration this poor friar was in, elevated his spirit a little too high to be contained within the bounds of reason : but before his delirium was perceived, he told his auditory one day ; that the true devotion of that people, and the care they had to come to hear his word preached, had been so acceptable to God and to the virgin, that they had vouchsafed to inspire him with the knowledge of an expedient, which he did not doubt but would make men happy and just even in this life ; and that the flesh should no longer lust against the spirit : but that he would not acquaint them with it at that present, because something was to be done on their parts to make them capable of this great blessing ; which was to pray zealously for a happy success upon his endeavours, and to fast and to visit the churches, to that end : therefore he desired them to come the Wednesday following to be made acquainted with this blessed expedient. You may imagine how desirous our people were, to hear some-

something more of this fifth monarchy. I will shorten my story, and tell you nothing of what crouding there was all night, and what quarrelling for places in the church; nor with what difficulty the Saffi, who were sent by the magistrate to keep the peace, and to make way for the preacher to get into the pulpit, did both: but up he got: and after a long preamble of desiring more prayers, and addressing himself to our senate to mediate with the Pope, that a week might be set apart for a jubilee and fasting three days all over the Christian world; to storm heaven with masses, prayers, fasting and alms to prosper his designs; he began to open the matter: that the cause of all the wickedness and sin, and by consequence of all the miseries and affliction which is in the world, arising from the enmity which is between God and the devil; by which means God was often cross'd in his intentions of good to mankind here and hereafter, the devil by his temptations making us uncapable of the mercy and favour of our creator: therefore he had a design (with the helps before-mentioned) to mediate with almighty God, that he

would

would pardon the devil; and. receive him into his favour again after fo long a time of banifhment and imprifonment; and not to take all his power from him, but to leave him fo much as might do good to man, and not hurt: which he doubted not but he would imploy that way, after fuch reconciliation was made, as his faith would not let him queftion. You may judge, what the numerous auditory thought of this: I can only tell you, that he had a different fort of company at his return from what he had when he came; for the men left him to the boys, who with great hoops inftead of acclamations brought him to the Gondola, which conveyed him to the Redentor; where he lodged: and I never had the curiofity to enquire, what became of him after.

Doft. I thank you heartily for this intermefs; I fee you have learn'd fomething in England: for, I affure you, we have been thefe twenty years turning this, and all ferious difcourfes into ridicule. But yet your fimilitude is very pat: for in every parliament that has been in England thefe fixty years, we have had notable contefts be-

tween

tween the feed of the ferpent and the feed of the woman.

Eng. Gent. Well, fir, we have had a Michael here in our age, who has driven out Lucifer, and reftored the true deity to his power : but where omnipotency is wanting, (which differs the Frier's cafe and mine,) the devil of civil war and confufion may get up again ; if he be not laid by prudence and virtue, and better conjurers than any we have yet at court.

Noble Ven. Well, gentlemen, I hope you have pardoned me for my farce : but, to be a little more ferious, pray tell me how you will induce the king to give up fo much of his right as may ferve your turn ? Would you have the parliament make war with him again ?

Eng. Gent. There cannot, nor ought to be, any change but by his majefty's free confent : for befides, that a war is to be abhorred by all men that love their country ; any conteft of that kind in this cafe (viz. to take away the leaft part of the king's right) could be juftified by no man living. I fay befides that, a civil war has mifcarried in our days ; which was found-

ed

ed (at leaſt pretendedly) upon defence of the people's own rights : in which, although they had as clear a victory in the end, as ever any conteſt upon earth had, yet could they never reap the leaſt advantage in the world by it ; but went from one tyranny to another, from Barebone's parliament, to Cromwell's reign ; and from that, to a committee of ſafety : leaving thoſe grave men, who managed affairs at the beginning, amazed to ſee new men and new principles governing England : and this induced them to co-operate to bring things back, juſt where they were before the war. Therefore this remedy will be either none, or worſe than the diſeaſe : it not being now as it was in the barons time, when the lord who led out his men, could bring them back again when he pleaſed, and rule them in the mean time, being his vaſſals : but now there is no man of ſo much credit, but that one who behaves himſelf bravely in the war, ſhall out-vye him ; and, poſſibly, be able to do what he pleaſes with the army and the government : and in this corrupt age, it is ten to one, he will rather do hurt than good with the power he acquires. But becauſe

you

you afk me how we would perfwade the king to this ? I anfwer ; by the parliament's humbly remonftrating to his majefty, that it is his own intereft, prefervation, quiet and true greatnefs, to put an end to the diftractions of his fubjects ; and that it cannot be done any other way : and to defire him to enter into debate with fome men authorized by them, to fee if there can be any other means than what they fhall offer to compofe things : if they find there may, then to embrace it ; otherwife, to infift upon their own propofals : and if in the end they cannot obtain thofe requefts, which they think the only effential means to preferve their country, then to beg their difmiffion ; that they may not ftay, and be partakers in the ruin of it. Now, my reafons why the king will pleafe to grant this after the thorough difcuffing of it, are two. Firft, becaufe all great princes have ever made up matters with their fubjects upon fuch contefts, without coming to extremities. The two greateft and moft valiant of our princes, were Edward the firft, and his grandchild Edward the third : thefe had very great demands made them by parliaments,

ments, and granted them all; as you may see upon the statute-book. Edward the second, and Richard the second, on the contrary, refused all things till they were brought to extremity. There is a memorable example in the Greek story of Theopompus, king of Sparta; whose subjects finding the government in diforder for want of some persons that might be a check upon the great power of the king, proposed to him the creation of the Ephores (officers who made that city fo great and famous afterwards.) The king finding by their reasons, which were unanswerable, (as I think ours now are,) that the whole government of Sparta was near its ruin without such a cure; and considering that he had more to lofe in that diforder than others, freely granted their defires: for which being derided by his wife, who afked him what a kind of monarchy he would leave to his fon? He anfwered; a very good one, because it will be a very lafting one. Which brings on my fecond reason, for which I believe the king will grant thefe things; because he cannot any way mend himself, nor his condition, if he do not.

Noble

Noble Ven. You have very fully convinced me of two things: firft, that we have no reafon to expect or believe that the parliament will ever increafe the king's power: and then, that the king cannot by any way found himfelf a new and more abfolute monarchy, except he can alter the condition of property: which I think we may take for granted to be impoffible. But yet, I know not why we may not fuppofe that (although he cannot eftablifh to all pofterity fuch an empire) he may, notwithftanding, change the government at the prefent; and calling parliaments no more, adminifter it by force, (as it is done in France,) for fome good time.

Eng. Gent. In France it has been a long work: and although that tyranny was begun, as has been faid, by petition from the ftates themfelves not to be affembled any more; yet the kings fince, in time of great diftraction, have thought fit to convocate them again: as they did in the civil wars thrice, once at Orleans, and twice at Blois. I would not repeat what I have fo tedioufly difcourfed of concerning France already; but only to intreat you to remember

ber that our nation has no such poor and numerous gentry, which draw better revenues from the king's purse, than they can from their own estates : all our country people consisting of rich nobility and gentry, of wealthy yeomen, and of poor younger brothers ; who have little or nothing, and can never raise their companies, if they should get commissions, without their elder brother's assistance amongst his tenants, or else with the free consent and desire of the people ; which, in this case, would hardly be afforded them. But we will suppose there be idle people enough to make an army, and that the king has money enough to arm and raise them : and I will grant too, to avoid tediousness (although I do not think it possible) that the people will at the first for fear, receive them into their houses and quarter them against law ; nay, pay the money, which shall be by illegal edicts imposed upon the subjects to pay them : yet is it possible an army can continue any time to enslave their own country ? Can they resist the prayers, or the curses, of their fathers, brothers, wives, mothers, sisters, and of all persons wherever they frequent ? Upon
this

this account, all the Greek tyrants were of very fhort continuance : who being in chief magiftracy and credit in their common-wealths, by means of foldiers and fatellites, ufurped the foveraignty. But did ever any of them, excepting Dionyfius, leave it to his fon? who was driven out within lefs than a year after his father's death. Many armies of the natives have deftroyed tyrannies : fo the Decemvirate was ruined at Rome, and the Tarquins expelled before that. Our own country has been a ftage, even in our time, where this tragedy has been fufficiently acted : for the army, after the war was done, fearing the monarchy fhould be reftored again, held counfels ; got agitators ; and though there were often very fevere executions upon the ring-lead-ers, did at length by their perfervance ne-ceffitate their officers to join with them, (having many good headpieces of the party to advife them ;) and fo broke all treaties. And the parliament adhering to a fmall party of them who confented to lay afide kingly go-vernment, they afterwards drove them away too; fearing they would continue to govern by an Oligarchy. I am far from approving the

way

way they ufed ; in which they broke all laws divine and humane, political and moral : but I urge it only to fhew how eafily an army of natives is to be deluded with the name of liberty ; and brought to pull down any thing, which their ring-leaders tell them tends to enflaving their country. 'Tis true, this army was afterwards cheated by their general ; who without their knowledge, (much lefs confent,) one morning fuddenly made himfelf tyrant of his country. It is true, that their reputation (not their arms) fupported him in that ftate for fome time ; but it is as certain that they did very often, and to the laft, refufe to be inftrumental to levy moneys, though for their own pay : and fo he, againft his will, was fain to call from time to time parliamentary conventions. And it is moft certain, that he did, in the ficknefs of which he died, often complain that his army would not go a ftep farther with him : and, *de facto*, fome months after his death, they did dethrone his fon, and reftore the remainder of the old parliament ; upon promife made to them in fecret, (by the demogogues of that affembly,) that a coma commonwealth fhould be fpeedily framed and fettled.

Noble Ven. Sir, I am fatisfied that an army raifed here on a fudden, and which never faw an enemy, could not be brought to act fuch high things for the ruin of their own government; nor poffibly, would be any way able to refift the fury and infurrection of the people: but what fay you of a foreign army, raifed by your king abroad, and brought over, whofe officers and foldiers fhall have no acquaintance or relations amongft the people here?

Eng. Gent. All forces of that kind muft be either auxiliaries, or mercenaries. Auxiliaries, are fuch as are fent by fome neighbour prince or ftate, with their own colours, and paid by themfelves; though poffibly, the prince who demands them may furnifh the money. Thefe ufually return home again, when the occafion for which they were demanded is over: but whether they do or not, if they be not mixed and over-ballanced with forces which depend upon the prince who calls them, but that the whole weight and power lies in them; they will certainly, firft or laft, feize that country

country for their own foveraign. And as for mercenaries ; they muft be raifed ('tis true) with the money of the prince who needs them, but by the authority and credit of fome great perfons who are to lead and command them : and thefe, in all occafions, have made their own commander prince ; as F. Sforza at Milan drove out by this trick the Vifconti, ancient dukes of that ftate ; and the Mamalukes in Egypt made themfelves a military commonwealth. So that the way of an army here, would either be no remedy at all ; or one very much worfe than the difeafe, to the prince himfelf.

Noble Ven. Well, fir, I begin to be of opinion, that any thing the king can grant the parliament (efpecially fuch a parliament as this is, which confifts of men of very great eftates and fo can have no intereft to defire troubles) will not be fo inconvenient to him, as to endeavour to break the government by force. But why may he not, for this time (by foothing them and offering them great alliances abroad for the intereft of England, and ballancing matters in Europe more even than they have been ;

M   and

and, in fine, by offering them a war with the French, to which nation they have fo great a hatred ;) lay them afleep, and get good ftore of money ; and ftave off this fevere cure you fpeak of, at leaft for fome time longer ?

Eng. Gent. There has been fomething of this done too lately ; and there is a gentleman lies in the tower, who is to anfwer for it. But you may pleafe to underftand, that there is fcarce any amongft the middle fort of people, much lefs within the walls of the houfe of commons, who do not perfectly know, that we can have no alliance with any nation in the world that will fignifie any thing to them, or to our felves, till our government be redreffed and new modelled : and therefore, though there were an army landed in this ifland, yet that we muft begin there ; before we are fit to repulfe them, or defend our felves. And the fear and fenfe of this people, univerfally, is ; that if we fhould have any war, either for our own concerns, or for thofe of our allies, whilft matters remain as they do at home, it would certainly come to this pafs : that either being beaten, we fhould fubject this

this kingdom to an invasion, at a time when we are in a very ill condition to repell it ; or else, if we were victorious, that our courtiers and counsellors *in fragrante* (or as the French cry *d'emble*) would employ that mettle and good fortune, to try some such conclusions at home, as we have been discoursing of. And therefore, if any war should be undertaken without parliament ; you would see the people rejoyce as much at any disaster our forces should receive, as they did when the Scots seized the four northern counties, in 1639 ; or, before that, when we were beaten at the isle of Rhee ; or when we had any loss in the last war with Holland. And this joy is not so unnatural as it may seem to those who do not consider the cause of it : which is the breach of our old government, and the necessity our governors are under to make some new experiments ; and the fear we are in, that any prosperity may make them able to try them, either with effect, or at least with impunity. Which consideration made a court-droll say lately to his majesty, (who seemed to wonder why his subjects hated the French so much ;) sir, it

is

is becaufe you love them, and efpoufe their intereft ; and if you would difcover this truth clearly, you may pleafe to make war with the king of France ; and then you fhall fee, that this people will not only love them, take their parts, and wifh them fuccefs : but will exceedingly rejoyce, when they are victorious in finking your fhips, or defeating your forces. And this is fufficient to anfwer your propofal for alliances abroad, and for a war with France. Befides this (to wind all up in a word) it is not to be imagined ; that fo good and wife a prince as we have at this time fhould ever be induced, when he comes to underftand perfectly his own condition, to let his own intereft (granting his power to be fo, which is very falfe) conteft with the fafety and prefervation of his people ; fór which only it was given him : or that he will be any way tenacious of fuch prerogatives, as now by a natural revolution of political circumftances are fo far from continuing ufeful to his governing the people, that they are the only remora and obftacle of all government, fettlement, and order. For his majefty muft needs know, that all forms of regulat-

ing

ing mankind under laws were ordained, by God and man, for the happinefs and fecurity of the governed ; and not for the intereft and greatnefs of thofe who rule : unlefs where there is *melior natura* in the cafe. So God governs man, for his own glory only ; and men reign over beafts, for their own ufe and fervice. But where an abfolute prince rules over his own fervants, whom he feeds and pays, (as we have faid;) or the mafter of a great and numerous family governs his houfhold ; they are both bound, by the law of God and nature, and by their own intereft, to do them juftice ; and not *infævire*, or tyrannize over them, more than the neceffity of preferving their empire and authority requires.

Doct. But fir, confidering the difficulty which will be found in the king, and poffibly in the parliament too, to come up to fo great an alteration at the firft ; and the danger that may happen by our remaining long in this unfettled condition, which does hourly expofe us to innumerable hazards, both at home, and from abroad ; why may we not begin, and lay the foundation now, by removing all his majefty's prefent council, by

parlia-

parliament? Which is no new thing; but hath been often practifed, in many kings reigns.

Eng. Gent. Firft, the council (that is, the privy council, which you mean) is no part of our government; as we may have occafion to fhew hereafter: nor is the king obliged by any fundamental law, or by any act of parliament, to hearken to their advice; or fo much as to afk it: and if you fhould make one on purpofe, befides that it would not be fo effectual as what we may propofe, it would be full as hard to go down either with king or parliament. But befides all this, you would fee fome of thefe counfellors fo nominated by parliament, perhaps, prove honeft; and then they would be forced to withdraw, as fome lately did; becaufe they found, I fuppofe, that till the adminiftration be alter'd, it is impoffible that their counfels can be embraced; or any thing be acted by them which may tend to the good of their country. Thofe, who have not fo great a fenfe of honour and integrity, will be prefently corrupted by their own intereft; whilft the prince is left in poffeffion of all thofe baits and means to anfwer fuch mens expectations: it being

most

moft certain, that if you have a mufty veffel, and by confequence diflike the beer
which comes out of it, and draw it out;
caufing the barrel to be immediately fill'd
with good and found liquor : it is certain
by experience, that both your new drink,
and all that ever you fhall put into the
cafk, till it be taken in pieces, and the pipes
fhaved and new-model'd, will be full as
mufty and unfavoury as the firft which you
found fault with.

Noble Ven. Now, fir, I think we are
at an end of our queftions : and I for my
part am convinced, that as the king cannot better himfelf any way by falling out
with his people at this time ; fo that his
goodnefs and wifdom is fuch, that he will
rather chufe to imitate the moft glorious
and generous of his predeceffors ; as Edward the firft, and Edward the third ; than
thofe who were of lefs worth, and more
unfortunate ; as Edward the fecond, and
Richard the fecond. And therefore we are
now ready to hear what you would think
fit to afk of fo excellent a prince.

Eng. Gent. I never undertook to be fo
prefumptuous : there is a parliament to fit

M 4   fpeedily,

speedily, and certainly they are the fitteft
every way to fearch into fuch matters ; and
to anticipate their wifdom would be unreafonable, and might give them juft offence.
But becaufe all this tittle-tattle may not go
for nothing, I fhall prefume to give you
my thoughts how the cure muft be wrought,
without defcending to particulars. The
caufe immediate (as we have faid) of our
difeafe, is the inexecution of our laws : and
it is moft true, that when that is alter'd for
the better, and that all our laws are duly
executed, we are in health. For as we can
never have the entire benefit of them, till
our government is upon a right bafis ; fo
whenever we enjoy this happinefs, to have the
full benefit of thofe conftitutions which were
made by our anceftors for our fafe and orderly
living, our government is upon a right bafis :
therefore we muft enquire into the caufe, why
our laws are not executed ; and when you
have found and taken away that caufe, all
is well. The caufe can be no other than
this, that the king is told, and does believe, that moft of thefe great charters or
rights of the people, of which we now
chiefly treat, are againft his majefty's in
                                    tereft ;

tereſt; though this be very falſe (as has been
ſaid) yet we will not diſpute it at this time,
but take it for granted : ſo that the king
having the ſupreme execution of the laws
in his hand, cannot be reaſonably ſuppoſed
to be willing to execute them whenever
he can chuſe whether he will do it or no ;
it being natural for every man not to do
any thing againſt his own intereſt when he
can help it. Now when you have thought
well what it ſhould be that gives the king
a liberty to chuſe whether any part of the
law ſhall be current or no ; you will find,
that it is the great power the king enjoys in
the government : when the parliament hath
diſcovered this, they will no doubt demand
of his majeſty an abatement of his royal prerogative in thoſe matters only which concern our enjoyment of our all, that is our
lives, liberties and eſtates ; and leave his
royal power entire and untoucht, in all the
other branches of it. When this is done,
we ſhall be as if ſome great hero had performed the adventure of diſſolving the in-
chantment, we have been under ſo many
years ; and all our ſtatutes from the higheſt
to the loweſt, from Magna Charta to that
for burying in woollen, will be current :

and

and we fhall neither fear the bringing in popery, nor arbitrary power in the intervals of parliament ; neither will there be any diffenfions in them ; all caufes of factions between the country and court party being entirely abolifht ; fo that the people fhall have no reafon to diftruft their prince, nor he them.

Doct. You make us a fine golden age : but after all this, will you not be pleafed to fhew us a fmall profpect of this Canaan, or country of reft ? Will you not vouchfafe to particularize a little, what powers there are in the king, which you would have difcontinued ? Would you have fuch prerogatives abolifhed, or placed elfewhere ?

Eng. Gent. There can be no government, if they be abolifhed. But I will not be like a man who refufes to fing amongft his friends at their intreaty, becaufe he has an ill voice ; I will rather fuffer my felf to be laught at by you in delivering my fmall judgment in this matter : but ftill with this proteftation, that I do believe that an infinity of men better qualified than my felf for fuch fublime matters, and much more the houfe of commons, who reprefent the wifdom as well as the power of this

king.

kingdom, may find out a far better way than my poor parts and capacity can suggest. The powers then which now being in the crown do hinder the execution of our laws, and prevent by consequence our happiness and settlement, are four. First, the absolute power of making war and peace, treaties and alliances with all nations in the world; by which means, by ignorant counsellors, or wicked ministers, many of our former kings have made confederations and wars, very contrary and destructive to the interest of England: and by the unfortunate management of them, have often put the king in great hazard of invasion. Besides that, as long as there is a distinction made between the court party and that of the country, there will ever be a jealousy in the people; that those wicked counsellors, (who may think they can be safe no other way,) will make alliances with powerful princes, in which there may be a secret article by which those princes shall stipulate to assist them with forces upon a short warning to curb the parliament, and possibly to change the government. And this apprehension in the people will be the less

unrea-

unreasonable; because Oliver Cornwell, (the great pattern of some of our courtiers,) is notoriously known to have inserted an article in his treaty with cardinal Mazarin, during this king of France's minority, that he should be assisted with ten thousand men from France upon occasion, to preserve and defend him in his usurped government, against his majesty that now is; or the people of England; or in fine, his own army; whose revolt he often feared. The second great prerogative the king enjoys, is the sole disposal and ordering of the militia by sea and land, raising forces, garisoning and fortifying places, setting out ships of war, so far as he can do all this without putting taxations upon the people; and this not only in the intervals of parliament, but even during their session; so that they cannot raise the train-bands of the country or city to guard themselves, or secure the peace of the kingdom. The third point is; that it is in his majesty's power to nominate and appoint as he pleases, and for what time he thinks fit, all the officers of the kingdom that are of trust or profit, both civil, military, and ecclesiastical,

cal, (as they will be called,) except where there is *jus patronatus.* Thefe two laft powers may furnifh a prince who will hearken to ill-defigning counfellors, with the means either of invading the government by force, or by his judges and other creatures undermining it by fraud. Efpecially by enjoying the fourth advantage ; which is the laying out and imploying, as he pleafes, all the publick revenues of the crown or kingdom, and that without having any regard (except he thinks fit) to the neceffity of the navy, or any other thing that concerns the fafety of the publick. So that all thefe four great powers, as things now ftand, may be adoperated at any time, as well to deftroy and ruin the good order and government of the ftate ; as to preferve and fupport it, as they ought to do.

Noble Ven. But if you diveft the king of thefe powers, will you have the parliament fit always to govern thefe matters ?

Eng. Gent. Sir, I would not diveft the king of them ; much lefs would I have the parliament affume them, or perpetuate their fitting. They are a body more fitted to make laws, and punifh the breakers of

3 them,

them, than to execute them. I would have them therefore petition his majesty by way of bill, that he will please to exercise these four great magnalia of government, with the consent of four several councils to be appointed for that end, and not otherwise; that is, with the consent of the major part of them, if any of them dissent. In all which councils, his majesty, (or who he pleases to appoint) shall preside. The councils to be named in parliament; first all the number, and every year afterwards a third part: so each year a third part shall go out, and a recruit of an equal number come in; and in three years they shall be all new: and no person to come into that council, or any other of the four, till he have kept out of any of them full three years, being as long as he was in: and this I learnt from your Quarantia's at Venice. And the use is excellent: for being in such a circulation, and sure to have their intervals of power; they will neither grow so insolent as to brave their king, nor will the prince have any occasion to corrupt them; although he had the means to do it, which in this new model he cannot have. These

men

men in their feveral councils fhould have
no other inftructions, but to difpofe of all
things and act in their feveral charges, for
the intereft and glory of England ; and fhall
be anfwerable to parliament, from time to
time, for any malicious or advifed mifde-
meanor. Only that council which manages the publick revenue, fhall (befides a
very copious and honourable revenue which
fhall be left to his majefty's difpofal for his
own entertainment, as belongs to the fplen-
dor and majefty of the government) have
inftructions to ferve his majefty (if he pleafes
to command them, and not otherwife) in
the regulating and ordering his oeconomy
and houfhold : and if they fhall fee it neceffary, for extraordinary occafions of treating foreign princes and ambaffadors, or prefenting them, (and the like oftentation of
greatnefs) to confent with his majefty moderately to charge the revenue to that end,
I verily believe that this expedient is much
more effectual, than either the Juftitia of Arragon was, or the Ephores of Sparta : who
being to check the king almoft in every
thing, without having any fhare in his
counfels or underftanding them, could not
chufe

chufe but make a fullen pofture of affairs :
whereas thefe both feem, and really are, the
king's minifters ; only obliged by parliament to act faithfully and honeftly : to
which, even without that, all other counfellors are bound by oath. As for the
other council, now called the privy council, the king may ftill pleafe to continue to
nominate them at his pleafure ; fo they act
nothing in any matters properly within the
jurifdiction of thefe four councils ; but meddle with the affairs of merchants, plantations, charters, and other matters to which
the regal power extendeth. And provided
that his majefty call none of the perfons
employed in thefe other four councils, during their being fo ; nor that this council do
any way intermeddle with any affairs, criminal or civil, which are to be decided by
law ; and do belong to the jurifdictions of
other courts or magiftrates : they being no
eftablifhed judicatory, or congregation,
which either our government or laws do
take notice of ; (as was faid before,) but
perfons congregated by the king; as his
friends and faithful fubjects, to give him
their opinion in the execution of his regal
office.

office. As for example, the king does exercise, at this time, a negative voice as to bills prefented to him by the parliament; which he claims by right : no man ever faid that the privy council had a negative voice; yet former kings did not only afk their advice as to the paffing or not paffing of fuch bills ; but often decided the matter by their votes : which, although it be a high prefumption in them, when they venture to give him counfel contrary to what is given him by his greateft council, yet never any of them have been queftion'd for it ; being looked upon as private men who fpeak according to the beft of their cunning, and fuch as have no publick capacity at all. But if this be not fo, and that this council have fome foundation in law, and fome publick capacity ; I wifh in this new fettlement it may be made otherwife : and that his majefty pleafe to take their counfel in private, but fummon no perfons to appear before them ; much lefs give them authority to fend for in cuftody, or imprifon any fubject ; which may as well be done by the judges and magiftrates : who, if fecrecy be required, may as well be fworn to fecrecy as thefe gentlemen -

men ; and (I believe) can keep counfel as well, and give it too.

Noble Ven. But would you have none to manage ftate-affairs ? None imprifoned for fecret confpiracies, and kept till they can be fully difcovered ? You have made an act here lately, about imprifonments ; that every perfon fhall have his habeas corpus, I think you call it : fo that no man, for what occafion foever, can lie in prifon a-bove a night, but the caufe muft be reveal-ed, though there be great caufe for the con-cealing it.

Eng. Gent. This act you mention, (and a great many more which we have to the fame purpofe, that is againft illegal impri-fonments,) fhews, that for a long time the power over men's perfons has been exercifed (under his majefty) by fuch as were likely, rather to employ it ill than well : that is, would rather imprifon ten men for honour-able actions ; (fuch as ftanding for the peo-ple's rights in parliament, refufing to pay illegal taxes, and the like) than one for projecting and inventing illegal monopolies; or any other kind of oppreffing the people. This made, firft Magna Charta, then the

Petition

Petition of Right, and divers other acts besides this last, take that power quite away;
and make the law and the judges the
only difpofers of the liberties of our perfons. And it may be, when the parliament fhall fee the fruit of this alteration
we are now difcourfing of, and that ftate-
affairs are in better hands, they may think
fit to provide that a return or warrant of
imprifonment from one of thefe four councils, (which I fuppofe will have a power of
commitment given them as to perfons ap-
pearing delinquents before them) wherein
it fhall be expreffed ; that if the publick is
like to fuffer or be defrauded, if the matter be immediately divulged ; I fay in this
cafe, the parliament may pleafe to make it
lawful for the judge to delay the bailing of
him for fome fmall time : becaufe it is not
to be judged, that thefe counfellors, fo
chofen, and fo inftructed, and to continue
fo fmall a time, will ufe this power ill ; efpecially being accountable for any abufing
of it to the next parliament : and I fuppofe the parliament, amongft other pro-
vifions in this behalf, will require that there
fhall be a regifter kept of all the votes of
                                    thefe

thefe feveral councils, with the names as well of thofe who confented, as of fuch who diffented. And as to the former part of your queftion, whether I would have none to manage ftate-affairs? I think there are very few ftate-affairs, that do not concern either peace and war, and treaties abroad; the management of the armies, militia, and *poffe comitatus* at home; the management of all the publick monys, and the election of all officers whatfoever. The other parts of ftate-affairs, which are making and repealing of laws, punifhing high crimes againft the ftate, with levying and proportioning all manner of impofitions upon the people, this is referved to the parliament itfelf: and the execution of all laws, to the judges and magiftrates. And I can think of no other affairs of ftate than thefe.

Doct. Do you intend that the council for chufing officers fhall elect them of the king's houfhold, that is his menial fervants?

Eng. Gent. No; that were unreafonable. Except any of them have any jurifdiction in the kingdom; or any place or preheminence

hence in parliament annexed to such office : but in these things which concern the powers and jurisdictions of these several councils, (wherein *la guardia della libertà*, as Machiavil calls it, is now to be placed) I shall not presume to say any thing ; but assure your self, if ever it come to that, it will be very well digested in parliament : they being very good at contriving such matters, and making them practicable ; as well as at performing all other matters, that concern the interest and greatness of the kingdom.

Doct. I have thought, that the Ephores of Sparta were an admirable magistracy ; not only for the interest of the people, but likewise for the preservation of the authority of the kings, and of their lives too. For Plutarch observes, that the cities of Mesene and Argos had the same government with Lacedemon ; and yet for want of erecting such an authority as was in the Ephores, they were not only perpetually in broils amongst themselves, and for that reason ever beaten by their enemies ; (whereas the Spartans were always victorious ;) but even their kings were the most miserable;

of

of men : being often called in question judicially, and so lost their lives ; and many of them murdered by insurrections of the people. And at last, in both these cities, the kings were driven out ; their families extirpated ; the territory new divided ; and the government turn'd into a Democracy. And I ever thought that this expedient you propose, (for I have heard you discourse of it often before now,) would prove a more safe and a more noble reformation, than the institution of the Ephores was : and that a prince who is a lover of his country; who is gracious, wise and just, (such a one as it has pleased God to send us at this time ;) shall be ten times more absolute when this regulation is made, than ever he was or could be before : and that whatsoever he proposes in any of these councils will be received as a law, nay as an oracle : and, on the other side, ill and weak princes shall have no possibility of corrupting men ; or doing either themselves, or their people, any kind of harm or mischief. But have you done now ?

Eng. Gent. No, sir ; when this provision is made for the execution of the laws,

whic

which I think very effectual, (not to say infallible,) although it is not to be doubted,
but that there will be from time to time
many excellent laws enacted; yet two I
would have passed immediately. The one,
concerning the whole regulation of the
elections to parliament: which we need
very much; and no doubt but it will be
well done. That part of it which is necessary to go hand in hand with our settlement, and which indeed must be part of it,
is; that a parliament be elected every year
at a certain day, and that without any writ
or summons; the people meeting of course
at the time appointed in the usual place;
(as they do in parishes at the church-house
to chuse officers;) and that the sheriffs be
there ready to preside and to certifie the
election. And that the parliament so chosen shall meet at the time appointed; and
sit and adjourn, as their business is more or
less urgent; but still setting yet a time for
their coming together again. And if there
shall be a necessity (by reason of invasion,
or some other cause) for their assembling
sooner; then the king to call the counsellors of these four councils all together, and
with

with the confent of the major part of them, intimate their meeting fooner. But when the day comes for the annual meeting of another parliament, they muft be underftood to be diffolved in law, without any other ceremony ; and the new one to take their place.

Doct. I would have this confidered too, and provided for ; that no election fhould be made of any perfon who had not the majority of the electors prefent to vote for him : fo the writ orders it ; and fo reafon dictates. For elfe how can he be faid to reprefent the county, if not a fifth part have confented to his choice ? As happens fometimes ; and may do oftener : for where feven or eight ftand for one vacant place, (as I have known in our laft long parliament,) the votes being fet in columns, he who has had moft votes has not exceeded four hundred, of above two thoufand who were prefent.

Noble Ven. This is a ftrange way ! I thought you had put every man by himfelf, as we do in our government, and as I underftood they do in the houfe of commons, when-

when there is any nomination ; and then, if he has not the major part, he is rejected.

Eng. Gent. This is very material ; and indeed effential : but I make no doubt, but if this project fhould come in play in parliament, this and all other particulars (which would be both needlefs and tedious to difcourfe of here) will be well and effectually provided for. The next act I would have paffed, fhould be concerning the houfe of peers : that as I take it for granted, that there will be a claufe in the bill concerning elections, that no new beroughs fhall be enabled to fend members to parliament except they fhall be capacitated thereunto by an act ; fo it being of the fame neceffity as to the liberty of parliament, that the peers (who do and muft enjoy both a negative and deliberative voice in all parliamentary tranfactions, except what concern levying of money originally) be exempted from depending abfolutely upon the prince ; and that therefore it be declared by act, for the future, that no peer fhall be made but by act of parliament, and then that it be hereditary in his male line.

Noble Ven. I am not yet fully fatisfied how you can order your matters, concern-

N

ing

ing this house of peers : nor do I see, how the contests between the house of commons and them can be so laid asleep, but that they will arise again. Besides, the house of commons must necessarily be extreamly concerned to find the house of peers, (which consists of private persons, though very great and honourable ones,) in an instant, dash all that they have been so long hammering for the good of all the people of England, whom they represent. Were it not better, now you are upon so great alterations, to make an annual elective senate; or at least one wherein the members should be but for life, and not hereditary ?

Eng. Gent. By no means, sir ; the less change the better : and in this case, the metaphysical maxim is more true than in any, viz., *Entia non sunt multiplicanda sine necessitate :* for great alterations fright men, and puzzle them ; and there is no need of it at all in this case. I have told you before, that there is a necessity of a senate ; and how short this government would be without it ; and how confused in the mean time. The Roman senate was hereditary amongst the Patricii; except the Censor left any of

them

them out of the roll during his magistracy, for some very great and scandalous offence: and in that case too there was an appeal to the people, as in all other causes; witness the case of Lucius Quintius, and many others. To shew that there can be no need of such a change here as you speak of, you may please to consider; that all differences between the several parts of any government, come upon the account of interest. Now when this settlement is made, the house of peers and the house of commons can have no interest to dissent: for as to all things of private interest, (that is, the rights of peers, both during the sitting of parliaments, and in the intervals,) is left to their own house to judge of; as it is to the house of commons, to judge of their own privileges. And as for the contest of the peers jurisdiction as to appeals from courts of equity; (besides that I would have that settled in the act which should pass concerning the lords house,) I believe it will never happen more, when the government is upon a right foundation; it having been hitherto fomented by two different parties: the court-party sometimes blowing up that difference

to

to break the seffion, left fome good bills for the people fhould pafs; or that the king, by rejecting them, might difcontent his people. To avoid which dilemma, there needed no more, but to procure fome perfon to profecute his appeal before the lords. Some honeft patriots afterwards poffibly might ufe the fame policy which they learnt from the courtiers, to quafh fome bill very deftructive in which they were out-voted in the commons houfe; otherwife it is fo far from the intereft of the commons to hinder appeals from courts of equity, that there is none amongft them but know we are almoft deftroyed for want of it. And when they have confidered well, and that fome fuch reformation as this fhall take place; they will find that it can never be placed in a more honourable and unbyas'd judicatory than this: and I could wifh, that even in the intermiffion of parliamentary feffions, the whole peerage of England, (as many of them as can conveniently be in town) may fit in their judicial capacities, and hear appeals in equity; as well as judge upon writs of error. Now as to your other objection, (which is indeed of great weight,) that the

the houfe of commons muft needs take it ill, that the lords fhould fruftrate their endeavours for the people's good by their negative ; if you confider one thing, the force of this objection will vanifh : which is, that when this new conftitution fhall be admitted, the lords cannot have any intereft or temptation to differ with the commons in any thing wherein the publick good is concerned ; but are obliged by all the ties in the world to run the fame courfe and fortune with the commons ; their intereft being exactly the fame : fo that if there be any diffenting upon bills between the two houfes, when each of them fhall think their own expedient conduces moft to the advantage of the publick, this difference will ever be decided by right reafon at conferences ; and the lords may as well convince the commons, as be convinced by them : and thefe contefts are and ever will be of admirable ufe and benefit to the commonwealth. The reafon why it is otherwife now, and that the houfe of peers is made ufe of to hinder many bills from paffing, that are fuppofed to be for the eafe of the people, is ; that the great counfellors and officers which fit

N 3

in

in that houfe do fuggeft, (whether true or
falfe,) that it is againft his majefty's will
and intereft that fuch an act fhould pafs ;
whereupon it has found obftruction.   But
hereafter, if our expedient take place, it
cannot be fo ; firft, becaufe our king himfelf
cannot have any defigns going (as was
proved before) which fhall make it his advantage to hinder any good intended his
people, whofe profperity then will be his
own ; and then, becaufe in a fhort time the
peers, being made by act of parliament,
will confift of the beft men of England both
for parts and eftates ; and thofe who are already made, if any of them have fmall eftates,
the king, (if he had the intereft,) would not
have the means to corrupt them : the publick moneys, and the great offices being to
be difpenfed in another manner than formerly : fo their lordfhips will have no motive in the world to fteer their votes and
counfels, but their own honour and confcience, and the prefervation and profperity
of their country.   So that it would be both
needlefs and unjuft to pretend any change
of this kind.   Befides, this alteration in the
adminiftration of our government being propoſed

-pofed to be done by the unanimous confent of king, lords, and commons, and not otherwife, it would be very prepofterous to believe, that the peers would depofe themfelves of their hereditary rights ; and betake themfelves to the hopes of being elected. It is true, they have loft the power they had ever the commons; but that has not been taken from them by any law, no more than it was given them by any, but is fallen by the courfe of nature ; as has been fhewn at large. But though they cannot lead the commons by their tenures as formerly, yet there is no reafon or colour that they fhould lofe their co-ordination ; which I am fure they have by law, and by the fundamental conftitution of the government : and which is fo far from being prejudicial to a lafting fettlement, (as was faid,) that it infinitely contributes to it ; and prevents the confufion which would deftroy it. If I fhould have propofed any thing in this difcourfe, which fhould have intrenched upon the king's hereditary right ; or that fhould have hindred the majefty and greatnefs of thefe kingdoms from being reprefented by his royal perfon ;

I

I should have made your story of the capuchine fryar very applicable to me.

Noble Ven. I see you have not forgiven me that novel yet : but pray give me leave to aſk you one queſtion. Why do you make the election of great officers, to be by a ſmall ſecret council ? That had been more proper for a numerous aſſembly ; as it is in moſt commonwealths.

Eng. Gent. It is ſo in Democracies, and was ſo in Sparta ; and is done by your great council in Venice : but we are not making ſuch a kind of government, but rectifying an ancient monarchy ; and giving the prince ſome help in the adminiſtration of that great branch of his regality : beſides it is ſufficient, that our parliament chuſes theſe councils ; (that is always underſtood, the lords and commons, with the king's conſent.) Beſides, it is poſſible that if ſuch a regulation as this come in debate amongſt them, the parliament will reſerve to itſelf the approbation of the great officers ; as chancellor, judges, general officers of an army, and the like ; and that ſuch ſhall not have a ſettlement in thoſe charges, till they are accordingly allowed of ; but may in the
mean

mean time exercise them. As to particulars, I shall always refer you to what the parliament will judge fit to order in the case : but if you have any thing to object, or to shew in general, that some such regulation as this cannot be effectual towards the putting our distracted country into better order ; I shall think my self oblig'd to answer you : if you can have patience to hear me, and are not weary already ; as you may very well be.

Noble Ven. I shall certainly never be weary of such discourse ; however I shall give you no further trouble in this matter : for I am very fully satisfied, that such reformation, (if it could be compassed ;) would not only unite all parties ; but make you very flourishing at home, and very great abroad. But have you any hopes that such a thing will ever come into debate ? What do the parliament-men say to it ?

Eng. Gent. I never had any discourse to this purpose, either with any lord, or member of the commons house ; otherwise than as possibly some of these notions might fall in, at ordinary conversation : for I do not intend to intrench upon the office of God, to teach our senators wisdom. I have
known

known fome men fo full of their own notions, that they went up and down, fput-
tering them in every man's face they met.
Some went to great men during our late
troubles; nay, to the king himfelf; to offer their expedients from revelation. Two
men I was acquainted with, of which one
had an invention to reconcile differences in
religion; the other, had a projeƈt for a
bank of lands to lye as a fecurity for fums of
money lent: both thefe were perfons of
great parts and fancy; but yet fo troublefome at all times, and in all companies,
that I have often been forced to repeat an
excellent proverb of your country : " God
" deliver me from a man that has but one bu-
" finefs ! " And I affure you there is no man's
reputation that I envy lefs, than I do that
of fuch perfons; and therefore you may
pleafe to believe, that I have not imitated
them in fcattering thefe notions; nor can I
prophefy, whether any fuch apprehenfions
as thefe will ever come into the heads of
thofe men, who are our true phyficians.
But yet to anfwer your queftion, and give
you my conjeƈture ; I believe that we are
not ripe yet for any great reform. Not
only

only becaufe we are a very debauch'd peeple; I do not only mean that we are given to whoring, drinking, gaming and idlenefs; but chiefly that we have a politique debauch, which is a neglect of all things that concern the publick welfare, and a fetting up our own private interest againft it : I fay, this is not all ; for then the polity of no country could be redreft : for every commonwealth that is out of order, has ever all thefe debauches we fpeak of, as confequences of their loofe ftate. But there are two other confiderations which induce me to fear that our cure is not yet near. The firft is ; becaufe moft of the wife and grave men of this kingdom are very filent, and will not open their budget upon any terms : and although they diflike the prefent condition we are in as much as any men, and fee the precipice it leads us to, yet will never open their mouths to prefcribe a cure ; but being afked what they would advife, give a fhrug, like your countrymen. There was a very confiderable gentleman as moft in England, both for birth, parts, and eftate ; who being a member of the parliament that was called in 1640, continued all the war

with

with them: and by his wifdom and eloquence (which were both very great) pro-
moted very much their affairs.   When the
factions began between the prefbyters and
independents, he joyned cordially with the
latter : fo far as to give his affirmative to
the vote of no addreffes : that is, to an order made in the houfe of commons, to fend
no more meffages to the king, nor to receive any from him.   Afterwards, when an
affault was made upon the houfe by the army, and divers of the members taken violently away and fecluded ; he difliking it,
though he were none of them, voluntarily
abfented himfelf ; and continued retired
(being exceedingly averfe to a democratical
government, which was then declared for,)
till Cromwell's ufurpation : and being infinitely courted by him, abfolutely refufed to
accept of any employment under him ; or
to give him the leaft counfel. When Cromwell was dead ; and a parliament called by
his fon, or rather by the army ; the chief
officers of which did, from the beginning,
whipfer into the ears of the leading members, that if they could make an honeft government, they fhould be ftood by (as the
word

word then was) by the army : this gentleman, at that time, neither would be elected into that parliament, nor give the leaft
advice to any other perfon that was ; but
kept himfelf ftill upon the referve. Infomuch that it was generally believed, that
although he had ever been oppofite to the
late king's coming to the government again,
though upon propofitions ; yet he might
hanker after the reftoration of his majefty
that now is. But the apprehenfion appeared
groundlefs when it came to the pinch : for
being confulted as an oracle by the then general Monk, whether he fhould reftore the
monarchy again or no ; he would make no
anfwer, nor give him the leaft advice : and,
de facto, hath ever fince kept himfelf from
publick bufinefs. Although, upon the banifhment of my lord of Clarendon, he was
vifited by one of the greateft perfons in
England ; and one in as much efteem with
his majefty as any whatfoever ; and defired
to accept of fome great employment near
the king : which he abfolutely refufing, the
fame perfon, not a ftranger to him, but well
known by him, begged of him to give his
advice how his majefty (who defired nothing

thing more than to unite all his people together, and repair the breaches which the
civil war had caused, now my lord Clarendon was gone who by his counsels kept
those wounds open) might perform that
honourable and gracious work : but still
this gentleman made his excuses. And,
in short, neither then, nor at any time before or after, (excepting when he sat in the
long parliament of the year 40 ;) neither
during the distracted times, nor since his
majesty's return, when they seemed more
reposed; would ever be brought, either by
any private intimate friend, or by any person in publick employment, to give the least
judgment of our affairs ; or the least counsel to mend them : though he was not shy
of declaring his dislike of matters as they
went. And yet this gentleman was not
only by repute and esteem a wise man,
but was really so ; as it appeared by his management of business, and drawing declarations, when he was contented to act; as also
by his exceeding prudent managing of his
own fortune, which was very great ; and
his honourable living and providing for his
family : his daughters having been all married

ried to the beſt men in England; and his eldeſt ſon to the moſt accompliſht lady in the world. I dare aſſure you, there are above an hundred ſuch men in England; though not altogether of that eminency.

Noble Ven. Methinks theſe perſons are altogether as bad an extreme as the loquacious men you ſpoke of before. I remember when I went to ſchool, our maſter, amongſt other common-places in the commendation of ſilence, would tell us of a Latin ſaying; that a fool while he held his peace did not differ from a wiſe man: but truly I think we may as truly ſay, that a wiſe man whilſt he is ſilent does not differ from a fool: for how great ſoever his wiſdom is, it can neither get him credit, nor otherwiſe advantage himſelf, his friend, nor his country. But let me not divert you from your other point.

Eng. Gent. The next reaſon I have to make me fear, that ſuch an expedient as we have been talking of will not be propoſed ſuddenly; is the great diſtruſt the parliament has of men. Which will make moſt members ſhy of venturing at ſuch matters, which being very new, at the firſt motion are

are not perfectly underſtood ; at leaſt to
ſuch as have not been verſed in authors who
have written of the politicks ; and therefore
the mover may be ſuſpected of having been
ſet on by the court-party to puzzle them ;
and ſo to divert, by offering new expedients,
ſome ſmart mettleſome debates they may be
upon concerning the ſucceſſion to the
crown, or other high matters. For it is
the nature of all popular councils (even the
wiſeſt that ever were, witneſs the people of
Rome and Athens, which Machiavil ſo much
extols) in turbulent times, to like diſcourſes
that heighten their paſſions and blow up
their indignation ; better than thoſe that
endeavour to rectifie their judgments, and
tend to provide for their ſafety. And the
truth is, our parliament is very much to be
excuſed, or rather juſtified, in this diſtruſt
they have of perſons ; ſince there hath been
of late ſo many and ſo ſucceſsful attempts
uſed by the late great miniſters, to debauch
the moſt eminent members of the commons
houſe, by penſions and offices : and therefore it would wonderfully conduce to the
good of the common-wealth, and to the
compoſing our diſordered ſtate ; if there
were

were men of fo high and unqueftionable a reputation, that they were above all fufpicion and diftruft, and fo might venture upon bold, that is (in this cafe) moderate counfels, for the faving of their country. Such men there were in the parliament of 1640 ; at leaft twenty or thirty : who having ftood their ground in feven parliaments before, which in the two laft kings reigns had been diffolved abruptly and in wrath ; and having refifted the fear of imprifonment and great fines for their love to England, as well as the temptation of money and offices to betray it ; both offer'd by the wicked counfellors of that age, tending both to the ruin of our juft rights and the detriment of their mafter's affairs : I fay, having conftantly and with great magnanimity and honour made proof of their integrity, they had acquired fo great a reputation, that not only the parliament, but even almoft the whole people ftuck to them ; and were fwayed by them in actions of a much higher nature than any are now difcourfed of ; without fear of being deferted, or as we fay, left in the lurch ; as the people of France often are by their grandees, when

O they

they raife little civil wars to get great places;
which as foon as they are offered, they lay
down their arms, and leave their followers to
be hang'd. But altho' thefe two reafons of
the filence of fome wife men, and the want
of reputation in others, does give us but a
fad profpect of our land of promife; yet we
have one confideration, which does
incourage us to hope better things ere long:
and that is the infallible certainty that we
cannot long continue as we are; and that we
can never meliorate, but by fome fuch principles as we have been here all this while
difcourfing of: and that without fuch helps
and fuccours as may be drawn from thence,
we muft go from one diftraction to another,
till we come into a civil war; and in the
clofe of it be certainly a prey to the king of
France, who (on which fide it matters not)
will be a gamefter and fweep ftakes at laft;
the world not being now equally ballanced
between two princes alike powerful, as it
was during our laft civil war: and if as well
this danger, as the other means to prevent
it, be underftood in time, (as no doubt it
will;) we fhall be the happieft and the greateft nation in the world in a little time: and

\   in

in the mean time, enjoy the beſt and moſt juſt eaſie government of any people upon earth. If you aſk me, whether I could have offer'd any thing that I thought better than this; I will anſwer you as Solon did a philoſopher, who aſkt him whether he could not have made a better government for Athens? Yes; but that his was the beſt, that the people would or could receive. And now I believe you will bear me witneſs; that I have not treated you as a wiſe man would have done, in ſilence : but it is time to put an end to this tittle-tattle, which has nauſeated you for three days together.

Noble Ven. I hope you think better of our judgments than ſo; but I believe you may very well be weary.

Doct. I am ſure the pariſh prieſts are often thanked for their pains, when they have neither taken half ſo much as you have, nor profited their auditory the hundredth part ſo much.

Eng. Gent. The anſwer to thank you for your pains, is always, thank you, ſir, for your patience; and ſo I do, very humbly, both of you.————

Noble

Noble Ven. Pray, fir, when do you leave the town?

Eng. Gent. Not till you leave the kingdom. I intend to fee you, if pleafe God, aboard the yacht at Gravefend.

Noble Ven. I fhould be afhamed to put you to that trouble.

Eng. Gen I fhould be much more troubled, if I fhould not do it; in the mean time I take my leave of you for this time, and hope to wait on you again to morrow. What, doctor, you ftay to confult about the convalefcence? Adieu to you both.

Doct. Farewell, fir.

Nullum numen abeft, fi fit prudentia.

F I N I S.